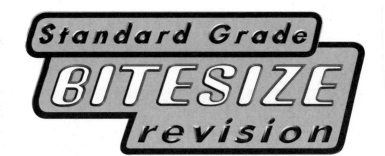

D1335264

Geography

Philip Duffy

Principal Teacher of Geography

St Thomas Aquinas Secondary School, Glasgow

With thanks to David Balderstone and Sheila King,
authors of GCSE Bitesize Revision: Geography,
first published 1998, reprinted 1999

Published by BBC Educational Publishing, White City,
201 Wood Lane, London W12 7TS
First published 1999, reprinted 2000 (twice)

Reprinted 2001 (twice)

© 1999 Philip Duffy/BBC Education,

ISBN: 0 563 46489 5

Designed by Cathy May (Endangered Species)

Printed in Great Britain by Bell and Bain, Glasgow

Contents

Introduction

◎ *Collect the words in bold and their definitions to compile your own glossary.*

About BITESIZEgeography

This book is a revision guide that has been put together to help you revise for your Standard Grade exams. In it you will find information on the main elements of the geography course, case studies, advice on how to answer exam questions and questions for you to practise your skills and knowledge through revision for your exam preparation. Throughout, there are words printed in **bold type** which you need to remember as part of your knowledge.

The book is called BITESIZEgeography because that's a good way to do your revision – in bitesize chunks. It is divided into small sections so you can work your way through the information and activities. The main aim is to make your revision as active as possible. If you have videoed the BBC Education Geography programmes, you can revise more actively by watching them and gathering more information to help with the activities, although the book is designed for use any time, anywhere and even if there is no television available. This book does not replace the notes and materials given to you by your teacher but it is an aid to help you to revise the information you have gathered over the length of the course.

❗ REMEMBER You can even go to the BBC web site on the internet for more help at http://www.bbc.co.uk/education/revision

What it can't do

This book doesn't cover every topic, example or case study in geography — that's just not possible. Nor can it cover every possible type of question to be found in an examination. But it will give you the confidence to approach questions in the right way and ensure you get the maximum marks available.

About Standard Grade

KEY TO SYMBOLS

📺 A link to the video

(?) Something to think about

◎ An activity to do

f foundation questions - very clear and easy to understand; worth 1-2 marks.

g general - worth 2, 3, or 4 marks.

C credit - more demanding, worth 4 or 6 marks.

Examination papers

Each paper will ask you questions on your Knowledge/Understanding (K/U) and Enquiry Skills (ES). You should answer all the questions on the paper.

Each paper will contain questions based on the three study themes:

■ **The Physical Environment**

■ **The Human Environment**

■ **International Issues**

A variety of question types will be included; most questions will be resource-based (maps, tables, graphs, sketches, cartoons) and at least one OS map-based question will be in each paper.

ƒ Foundation, **grades 5 and 6** - 1 hour 5 mins

- There are usually about 12 questions to answer in this paper.

- Questions are very clear and easy to understand and worth one or two marks.

- The questions will include maps, sketches, graphs, cartoons.

- You write your answers in the exam booklet in the spaces provided.

- You are asked to give short answers and explanations.

- The answer space given will give you a clue to how long your answer should be.

For example:

Reference Diagram Q9A: India's population

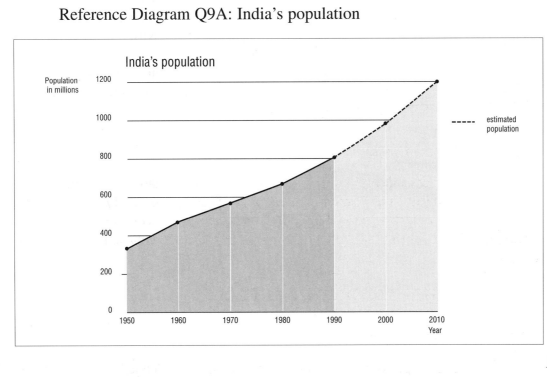

Marks

Look at the diagram above.

(a) Describe what has happened to the number of people in India between 1950 and 1990.

_____

_____

_____

_____

(2)

ⓖ General, **grades 3 and 4** - 1 hour 25 mins.

- There are usually about 10 questions to answer.

- Questions are very clear and easy to understand and worth 2, 3 or 4 marks.

- The questions will include maps, sketches, graphs, cartoons.

- You write your answers in the exam booklet in the spaces provided.

- Answers are longer and more detailed than in the Foundation paper.

- The answer space given and the marks for the question will give you a clue to how long your answer should be.

For example:

Reference Diagram Q1C: Types of transport in the Scottish Highlands

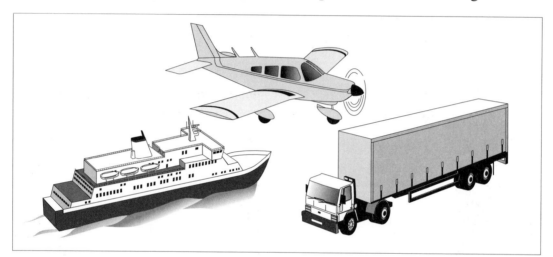

Marks

(b) Look at the diagrams above.

Explain why winter **weather** forecasts are important to **two** of the transport types shown.

Choice 1 _____

Reason _____

_____

_____

Choice 2 _____

Reason _____

_____

_____ **(4)**

©   Credit, **grades 1 and 2** - 2 hours

■ There are usually 8 questions to answer in this paper.

■ The questions are more demanding and worth 4 or 6 marks.

■ More complex sources (maps, sketches, graphs, cartoons) are used to test your knowledge and skills.

■ Unlike the F and G papers, you write your answers in a separate answer booklet.

■ Answers should be detailed.

■ The marks each question is worth will give you a clue to how detailed your answer should be.

For example:

! REMEMBER
Plan to spend more time on questions that are worth more marks.

---

5.   Study Reference Diagrams Q5A and Q5B and answer the question which follows

Reference Diagram Q5A: California – cities and physical features

Reference Diagram Q5B: California — population distribution

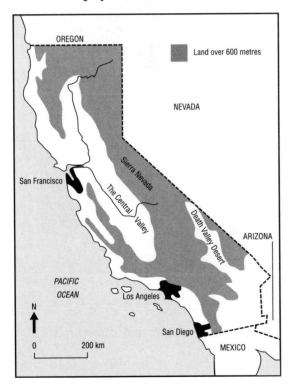

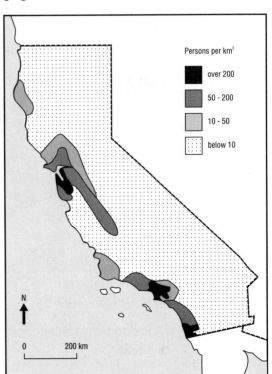

Describe in detail the relationship between physical features and population distribution in California.

Marks

(4) ES

Assessable elements

Knowledge/Understanding (K/U) — worth 40% of the marks in the exam

You have to remember some of the facts, ideas, processes and issues that you have studied and must be able to use these in answers to questions. Make sure you know what certain key words mean e.g. **erosion**, **deposition** (see page 36).

You will also be expected to show that you understand processes, patterns and features.

You might be asked to draw a diagram or sketch to show that you have understood this.

For example:

R E M E M B E R
Try to use geographical words in your answer.

8

Reference Diagram Q3A: An upland mixed farm in Scotland

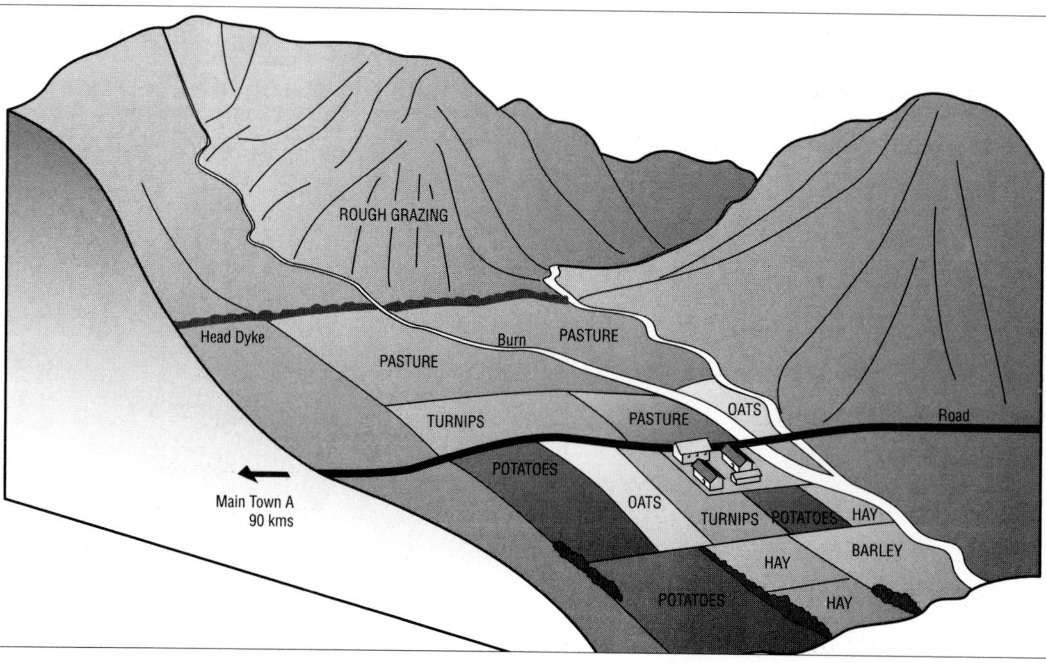

ROUGH GRAZING

Head Dyke Burn PASTURE

PASTURE

PASTURE

TURNIPS PASTURE OATS Road Main Town B 80 kms

POTATOES

Main Town A 90 kms

OATS

TURNIPS POTATOES HAY

HAY BARLEY

POTATOES HAY

Marks

(a) Look at Reference Diagram Q3A.

Describe the problems facing farmers in areas such as that shown in the diagram.

(4)

Enquiry Skills (ES)- worth 60% of the marks in the exam

REMEMBER In Enquiry Skills questions you are being asked to use the information supplied in the question.

Given information in the questions you will be able to:

■ state the main points and/or relationships of the information;

■ identify techniques for processing information and be able to justify your choice;

For example:

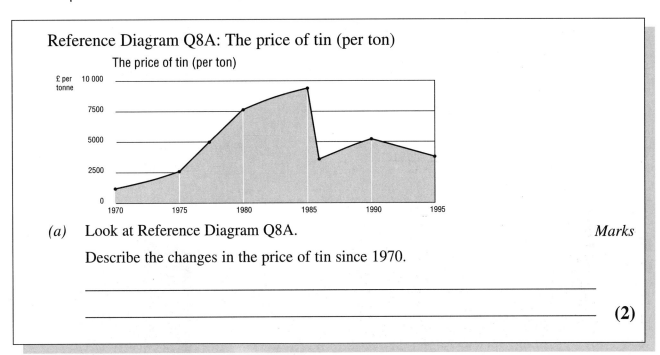

Reference Diagram Q8A: The price of tin (per ton)

The price of tin (per ton)

(a) Look at Reference Diagram Q8A.   *Marks*

Describe the changes in the price of tin since 1970.

_____

_____ **(2)**

■ identify techniques for gathering information and be able to justify your choice;

For example:

(d) You are carrying out a study of the two Industrial Areas **W** and **Z**. As part of your study you have decided to:

   (i) compare the types of industries in the two areas **and**

   (ii) find out how workers travel to their jobs.

For each of these, give a technique you would use to gather information.
You must give a different technique for each. Give a reason for each choice.   *Marks*

Types of industries _____

Reason _____

How workers travel to work _____

Reason _____ **(4)**

■ identify techniques for processing information and justify your choice.

For example:

Reference Table Q3B: Land-use on the farm (%)

Pasture	15	Cereals	10
Root Crops	20	Rough Grazing	55

(b) As part of a farm study you have collected the information shown in Reference Table Q3B.

Marks

Give **one** type of graph you would use to show this information **and** give a reason for your choice.

Choice _____

Reason _____

(2)

! REMEMBER Standard Grade examinations are not trying to catch you out. Questions may not be about places you have studied, but they will allow you to show what you know and can do in geography.

! REMEMBER Try to use geographical words when you are writing your answer, e.g. if you are describing places on a map, use compass directions: 'The river flows from the south west to the north east of the map'. Use place names or examples to impress the examiner.

Understanding the questions

Here are some words that are used in the Standard Grade questions. Do you know exactly what they are telling you to do?

Compare/Contrast - Identify and write down the things that are the same and are different between the features or places in the question.

Complete - You might be asked to finish off a diagram, map or graph.

Define - Describe or explain the meaning of something.

Describe - Write down things about what is shown on a map, table or graph.

Discuss - Usually requires a longer answer as you are describing and giving reasons or explaining arguments 'for' or 'against'.

Do you agree ?
Tick (✓) your choice   YES or NO
You are being asked to make a choice between the given answers.

Draw/Annotate - You might be asked to draw a sketch or diagram with labels to explain the formation of a feature e.g. **meander, corrie**

Explain (account for)/Justify/Give a reason/Give detailed reasons/Suggest reasons/Argue a point of view - Give reasons for the location or appearance of a feature.

Give your views - You might be asked to say what you think or what another person or group might think.

Identify - Name, locate, recognise or select a particular feature or features from a map, photograph or diagram.

Locate - Write down where a feature or place is.

Name, state or list - Write down accurate details or information.

Study/Look at - Look carefully at a map, diagram, sketch, table and think about what it shows.

Technique - Refers to either a gathering or processing technique.

Using map evidence (OS maps) You must give a 4 or 6-figure grid reference and/or mention a place, name or feature taken from the map.

With reference to (or refer to) examples that you have studied - You need to give detailed and specific information about the case study when you explain the reasons for a particular answer.

With the help of or **Using the information provided** - Be sure to use and mention examples from the information, e.g. tables and graphs in the paper.

What to revise?

The key to revising is to organise what you have studied into short notes, lists, sketches, diagrams and tables so that it is easier to remember. Short, well-organised notes help you to focus on the important ideas and facts.

There seems to be an awful lot to revise, but the points below will help you concentrate on the important elements that will get you marks in the exam:

■ the meaning of key geographical words and phrases;

■ information about and explanation of geographical ideas and processes, e.g. how a waterfall forms;

■ causes and effects; impacts of geographical processes and events, e.g. changes in birth and death rates;

■ similarities and differences between features and places, e.g. comparing old and new industrial areas;

■ attitudes and values of different interest groups, e.g. conflicts over the building of a new road;

■ alternative views, e.g. farmer and hill walker;

■ factors and characteristics, e.g. causes of migration;

■ advantages and disadvantages of different plans, e.g. out-of-town shopping centres;

■ arguments for and against different proposals, e.g. building of a quarry;

■ sketch maps and diagrams to show or explain features, e.g. how a **meander** is formed;

■ diagrams that help to show or explain how features may be formed, e.g. formation of a **corrie**.

It's more fun if you work with a friend. Ask each other questions on things you have revised.

REMEMBER If you are asked to describe a line graph, mention any *changes* to the line (rising, falling, level) and how quickly these changes take place (slowly rising, falling quickly, stayed level for some years).

11

REMEMBER In a question on a bar or pie chart, *compare* the size of the different bars or sectors and mention the relative importance of each (e.g. housing takes up 60% of the area).

REMEMBER In geography revision you are aiming to improve your understanding of geographical ideas and processes; improve your recall ('unlocking' your memory) during exams; learn how to adapt what you know to answer a wide range of questions.

Making revision notes

One of the main functions of revision in geography is to help you to learn important information about geographical ideas, processes, case studies and examples that you have studied. Making revision notes will help you to rework your class and other work so that there's a manageable amount of information to learn; and it's organised in a way that makes it easier to learn. Below is an example to show you how revision notes could be organised:

Each revision card has a clear title to remind you about the topic covered.

After the title start with a summary of the main ideas or themes covered on the sheet.

Explaining the geographical processes -reasons for rural-urban migration.

Consequences - in this case the problems resulting from the rapid growth of cities in LEDCs.

Useful information about places shown on the sketch map added as annotated notes

Key geographical words underlined or highlighted

Use sub-headings to help to structure the information that is to be learnt.

Useful facts

Organise information in lists to aid learning.

Facts about real places

A sketch map might help you to remember some of the important locations and places

---

Urbanisation (the growth of cities) in LEDC's
• Reasons for the growth of cities   • Possible solutions   • Impacts of growth

Main reasons for the growth of cities
Rural-urban migration

Push factors	pull factors
- to leave rural areas	-attractions of towns and cities
Fewer jobs	More jobs
Low wages	Higher wages
Poor health and education	Better schools
	Health services
Population pressure	Opportunities to improve standard of living
Unprofitable farming	

High rate of natural increase
High proportion of migrants are of child-bearing age;

High birth /lower death rates.

Rapid growth of Nairobi
1960 - popn. of 300 000
1985 - popn. of 875 000
1995 - popn. of 2 million

% of Nairobi's popn. living in squatter settlements
1960 - 7%   1985 - 35%
1995 - 50%

Problems resulting from this rapid growth
Not enough housing   growth of shanty towns and poor quality housing
Not enough jobs   many work in the 'informal sector' with low wages

• Traffic congestion and poor public transport • Poor sanitation • no sewerage or clean water supples in many shanty towns • disease and poor health

Possible solutions

1954   city authorities demolished shanty towns and tried to limit/control migration to Nairobi

1960-70 authorities refuse to provide basic services

1974   recognition of shanty towns (not demolished)

'Sites and services' scheme to provide some basic services eg. clean water supplies, sewerage and electricity

N

MATHARE RIVER

1960-70
CBD prospered as a result
of the rapid growth in the
Kenyan economy

KOROKOCHO   KARIOBANGI

1965 - 30,000 people
1980 - 90,000

DAGORETTI

NAIROBI RIVER

CBD

MATHARE VALLEY

0   3
Kms

MARSHLAND

Main shanty towns
of Nairobi

NGONG RIVER   KIBERIA

1972 Cholera epidemic in
Nairobi. Authorities provide
water to shanty towns within
3 days of outbreak

1974-85 Nairobi's
"sites and services" scheme
· small rent for a building site
· water, sewerage and electricity provided

NAIROBI GAME PARK

BITESIZEgeography

Practise Standard Grade questions

Try including one or two practice questions in your geography revision each week so that you practise using what you are revising. There are lots of questions in this book for you to try, and the correct answers are all at the back. Try doing this with a friend, too, then check your answers. Explain to each other why you included particular facts or examples.

REMEMBER In Standard Grade you must answer all questions.

Before exams

■ Be sure you know exactly where and when each paper is being held. You will have been given an exam timetable that will give you all the details. Note that some papers start at 9a.m.

■ Have breakfast before you leave home so you don't feel hungry or faint in the middle of an exam.

■ Arrive for each paper on time. You can be refused entry if you are late.

■ Check the list outside the exam room to locate your seat number.

■ Bring the necessary equipment: pens, pencils, ruler, rubber, sharpener...

REMEMBER Be on time for the exam.

Final moments

There are various things to do before you start the exam paper:

■ Listen carefully to the invigilator's instructions

■ Fill in your exam paper cover fully and accurately, making sure the exam paper is the one you should be sitting.

■ Read the instructions on the front of the exam paper.

■ Remember you have to answer all the questions in the paper.

■ Plan your time carefully. Too many students do not finish some questions or do not answer some of them at all.

■ Leave time at the end to check for careless mistakes.

Your answers

■ You have to answer *all* questions so just start at the front of the paper and work your way to the end.

■ Before you start answering a question make sure you have read it through and understand what you are being asked to do.

■ Write as quickly and as clearly as you can. Take care with your spelling.

■ Draw large, clearly labelled diagrams when asked.

■ Spend longer answering questions with more marks.

■ If you are unsure about a question, move on and come back to it later.

■ You may find that some questions are more difficult than others - don't give up.

REMEMBER Use real examples about real people and real places. Don't be vague, name examples, give facts and figures and use the correct geographical terms.

Enquiry skills - gathering techniques

The following techniques of gathering and processing information will be part of the geography exam. At **Foundation Level**, you will be asked to state a technique from a given short list. At **General Level**, you will be asked to name a technique(s) and justify your choice with a reason. At **Credit Level**, you will be asked to name a technique(s) and *justify* your choice(s) with reasons.

Gathering technique	Topic example	Reason for use
1 Extracting information from maps (and other sources)	- site of a settlement - land-use types or changes - land-use conflicts - weather data from satellite photos	- maps are a good store of information - information on location, links and features can be taken from maps - information on a map can be related to land-use and slope/soil - maps from different times can be used to compare changes
2 Fieldsketching	- industrial landscapes - river features - glacial features - farming landscape	- is more selective than a photograph - can be used to highlight the important/relevant information - can by used to compare with photo or map from the past
3 Measuring (rivers, weather)	- elements of the weather - river flow - river depth and width	- provides original data to be processed - source of precise/accurate information - comparing the water flow/speed across a river - measure weather elements over time to show changes
4 Recording observed information on a map (land-use, location, distribution)	- differing land values/uses - sphere of influence of a town/shop	- is a good way of storing observed information to be processed later - land-use, location, distribution, can be stored and be compared for relationships
5 Observing and recording (traffic and pedestrian flows, environmental quality, buildings, services, weather)	- traffic flow - elements of the weather - pedestrian flows - quality of the environment	- used to gather information at source - making notes in a field notebook - traffic and pedestrian flows on a grid sheet - entering weather data onto a data base - taking photos/video to show environmental quality - information can be processed, analysed, compared
6 Compiling and using questionnaires and interviews	- sphere of influence - land use conflicts - changes to a landscape/environment	- used to collect original information directly from people - up to date and accurate source of facts and opinions - means of collecting information about the past

Enquiry skills - processing techniques

Processing technique	Topic example	Reason for use
1 Classifying, tabulating, matrixing	- compare imports/exports - changes in crops grown over time	- ways of organising and presenting data/information - easier to make sense of information arranged in tables - can be studied or compared to show trends - matrixing is a good way of storing information to show possible relationships

2 Drawing graphs
  - bar graphs
  - line graph
  - pie chart
  - scatter graph
	- types of exports
	- temperature
	- land-use in a town
	- relationship between services and settlement size
		Bar graphs - used to compare information
		- can be used with maps to combine information with location
		- can be used to show +/- values
		Divided bar graphs - show relative importance of different parts
		Line graphs - show a trend or change over time
		- show amount or rate of change, steepness and degree of change
		Pie chart - shows how an amount is shared out
		- the relative importance of the parts/sectors can be put on a map to aid comparison between places
		Scatter graph - way of testing connection between two sets of data, e.g. relationship between GNP and infant mortality

3 Drawing maps	- land-use in the CBD of a city - sphere of influence - land-use on a farm - traffic/pedestrian flows	- means of showing links between features - selective way of showing information - way of showing information to indicate and reveal patterns, e.g. land-use in a city; location and distribution of shopping centres
4 Drawing cross-sections/ transects	- across a river valley - relationship between land-use and soil-type	- vertical representation of the contours on a map - height and shape is shown and the position of key features - allows comparison of data e.g. building use and land values from CBD to city edge
5 Annotating maps, graphs and field sketches	- river meanders - corrie - industrial landscape - farming landscape	- provides a sample of an area to bring out key features - enhances information - can be used to name and identify features - draws attention to relationships, patterns

Ordnance Survey (OS)

All three papers will have a question that involves the use of an OS map. The level of difficulty will depend on the paper.

What is expected

16

REMEMBER
Be specific. Give 4 or 6 positive grid references – they will impress the examiner.

You must:

■ be prepared to use any sort of map. The most common are Ordnance Survey maps at 1:25 000 and 1:50 000, but other types have been used, e.g. road and tourist maps.

■ be able to use the key of the map to identify symbols;

■ use the scale of the map to measure distance;

■ use the compass to give directions;

■ use 4-figure grid references (**F/G**) or 6-figure grid references (**G/C**)

■ use your knowledge of the human and physical environment to help you answer questions;

■ be able to recognise the following:

contours, spot heights, flat land, steep or gently sloping land
rivers, river features, glaciated features (U-shaped valley)
land used for farming, forestry, recreation, settlement, industry and communications - railways, roads (motorway, A class, B class, minor).
settlement patterns, e.g. CBD (Central Business District) old industrial areas (19th century); new industrial areas (20th century); old housing areas (19th century); new housing areas (20th century).

■ list advantages and/or disadvantages of one site for development compared to another;

■ list advantages and/or disadvantages of a site for development of housing, recreation, industry, roads, etc;

■ be able to use a transect/cross-section to locate places and land-uses on a map.

Mapwork-style questions

Here are some of the kinds of things you may be asked in mapwork questions and what is required in the replies.

- Match a glacial feature to its grid reference.

  For a large feature which fills the grid box, for example a large meander, give a 4-figure grid reference.

  For a smaller feature, for example a waterfall, use a 6-figure grid reference.

- Using map evidence, explain the growth of...

  This evidence must include names of places or features on the map with grid references.

- Describe the distribution of settlements ...

  Describe where the settlements are located, for example, avoiding lowland or highland, at a bridging-point, spread across the map.

- Which type of farming is likely to be practised at Farm Y?

  Identify as arable, sheep, etc.

- What are the advantages and disadvantages of ....?

  Describe both advantages and disadvantages.

- Why is Site X a good site for a new factory?

  Look at the map for evidence to support the following:

  large, flat, level site, with room for expansion, near houses for workers or shoppers and close to good transport links, e.g. a motorway.

  Use the opposite to describe why a site is not a good choice:

  small, hilly site, little room for expansion, far from houses for workers and shoppers to get to, poor roads with limited access for large lorries.

  Examples of these types of questions are included in the Exam questions sections of this book.

  There are two OS maps to look at on colour pages i-iv at the back of this book, and some questions to try on page 58 (Stirling) and page 92 (Fort William).

Good luck!

This section is about

- elements of, and instruments used, to measure the weather

- types of weather

- ways we collect weather information for forecasts

- how the weather affects people

📺 Key words

- **instruments**   see the FactZONE opposite

- **Beaufort scale**   used to estimate the speed or force of the wind by its effects on objects around us, e.g trees

- **warm front**   gives us prolonged, steady rain

- **cold front**   gives us heavy rain

- **isobars**   lines on a weather map joining places with the same pressure

- **low pressure**   isobars are close together. Brings unsettled weather with cloud, strong winds and rain in summer and winter

- **warm sector**   warm and dry air between the warm and cold fronts

- **anti-cyclones**   area of **high pressure** with winds blowing clockwise

Enquiry skills

Topic	Gathering technique	Processing technique
Elements	Observing and recording clouds, wind speed, visibility	classifying tabulating
	Measuring temperature, rainfall, wind speed and direction, sunshine, air pressure,	bar graphs line graphs wind rose
Weather maps and forecasts	Extracting information from satellite photos, radar images	
	Extracting information from TV, radio, newspapers, Internet	drawing maps tabulating
People and the weather	Interviewing people after a storm or during a drought	classifying tabulating graphs

FactZONE

(TV) Weather station

Measuring temperature

Element temperature
Instrument thermometer
Units degrees Celsius
Location Stevenson screen

maximum temperature

minimum temperature

Degrees

28
26
24
22
20
18
16
14
12
10
8
6
4
2
0

1 2 3 4 5 6 7 8 9 10
Days

Stevenson screen

double roof so that screen does not heat up

painted white to reflect sun's heat

door faces north to keep out direct sunlight

louvred or slatted sides let air pass through and keep out direct sunlight

Thermometer

minimum temperature   maximum temperature

alcohol vapour
alcohol
metal pin
metal pin
mercury

°C
-25
-20
-15
-10
-5
0
5
10
15
20
25
30
35
40

°C
40
35
30
25
20
15
10
5
0
-5
-10
-15
-20
-25

Measuring wind speed

Element wind speed
Instrument anemometer
Units kilometres per hour (km/h)
Location 10 metres above the ground

Anemometer

3 metal cups catch the wind and spin round

speedometer

003654
kms m

Measuring wind direction

Element wind direction
Instrument wind vane
Units compass points
Location in open away from buildings

Wind vane

arrow shows the direction the wind comes from

wind hits the metal strip, causing the wind vane to turn

W   S
N   E

several metres above the ground

NW   NE
W
SW   SE
S

Scale: 1 day = 1mm

Observing cloud cover

Element cloud
Units Oktas (eigths of the sky)
Location clear view of the sky above

Observing visibility

Element visibility
Units metres or kilometres
Location where you can see some distance

Measuring humidity

Element humidity
Instrument wet and dry bulb thermometers
Units percentage %
Location Stevenson screen

Dry bulb thermometer   Wet bulb thermometer

Temperature °C
35
30
25
20
15
10
5
0
-5
-10

saturated lint

water

Measuring rainfall

Element precipitation
Instrument rain gauge
Units millimetres (mm)
Location sunk into soil away from buildings

Rain gauge

copper cylinder
funnel
collecting bottle

30 cm

measuring jug

Measuring air pressure

Element air pressure
Instrument barometer/barograph
Units millibars (mb)
Location inside

Barograph

pressure sensitive arm with pen attached draws line onto graph paper

grass minimum thermometer

soil thermometer

Measuring sunshine

Element sunshine
Instrument sunshine recorder
Units hours
Location in open clear of shade

Sunshine recorder

glass ball

strip of card

Recording card

time of day

3 6 9 12 15 18 21

No burn marks, no sunshine

Burn mark shows that the sun was shining

Hours of sunshine

14
12
10
8
6
4
2
0

1 2 3 4 5 6 7 8 9 10
Days

(◎) *Use the diagram above and the key words list to help you to complete this table.*

Element	Instrument	Unit	Location
Temperature	Thermometer	Degrees Celsius	found in Stevenson screen
Precipitation			
Wind direction			
Wind speed			
Clouds			
Visibility			
Air pressure			
Sunshine			

! REMEMBER Learn the names of the instruments that measure weather. You may be asked to name them in an exam.

! REMEMBER Precipitation includes rain, snow, sleet, hail, frost, dew, fog and mist.

Air streams

People sometimes say that 'winds bring the weather'. Air masses are very large volumes of air with uniform temperature and humidity (e.g. they might be wet and warm or cold and dry). Where the air comes from and what it passes over influence the weather that the air mass brings. The air takes on some of the properties of the surfaces over which it travels. These properties influence the weather and climate of Britain.

◎ Complete the diagram below to show the names and characteristics of the main air masses that affect Britain's weather and climate.

Name of air mass: _____

Source region: _____

Characteristics: _____

Weather: _____

Name of air mass: _Arctic Maritime_

Source region: _Arctic Circle_

Characteristics: _cold and wet_

Weather: _snow in winter_

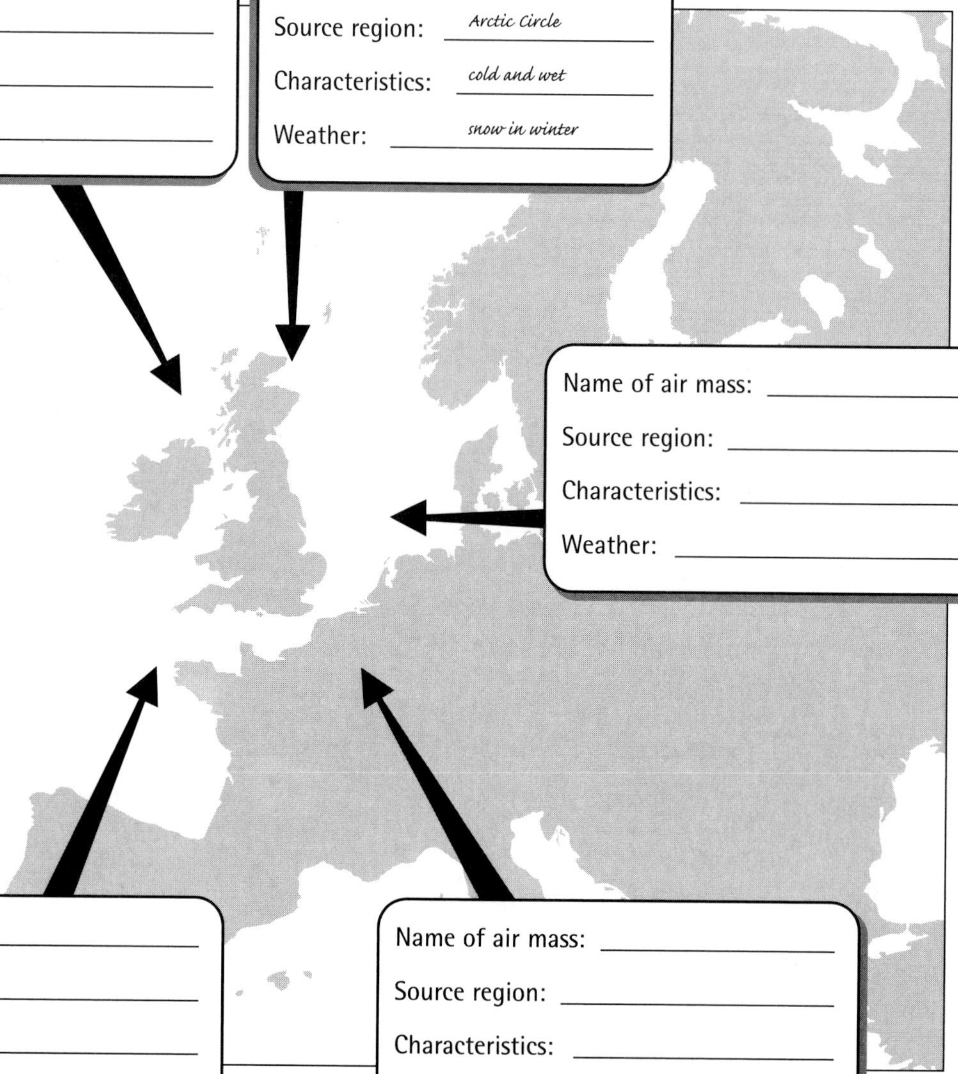

Use these words:

Polar maritime;Tropical maritime; Polar continental; Tropical continental.

Mid Atlantic; Greenland – Arctic Sea; North Africa; central Europe and Siberia.

Warm, moist air; wet and cold; cold in winter, hot in summer; hot, dry air.

Hot and dry in summer; mild, cloudy, rain; cool with heavy showers; very cold with some snow in winter, hot and dry in summer.

Name of air mass: _____

Source region: _____

Characteristics: _____

Weather: _____

Name of air mass: _____

Source region: _____

Characteristics: _____

Weather: _____

Name of air mass: _____

Source region: _____

Characteristics: _____

Weather: _____

Pressure and wind

Pressure refers to the weight of air pressing on the surface of the Earth and it is measured in **millibars (mb.)**. It is shown on weather maps by **isobars**. These are lines joining places of equal pressure (usually drawn at intervals of 4 or 8 millibars).

The diagrams on pages 22-23 show how pressure and wind are related. **Wind** is air moving between two areas of different pressure. Winds blow out from areas of high pressure towards areas of low pressure. On a weather map, winds blow parallel to the isobars. **Wind speed** is related to the distance over which the changes in pressure happen. The closer together the isobars are, the stronger the wind. You often hear weather forecasters talking about isobars being 'packed closely together' when they forecast strong winds. The **wind's direction** is always given as the compass direction which the wind blows from. The **prevailing wind** is the direction that the wind blows from most often.

◎ *Draw arrows on the diagram below to show the direction of the winds that you would expect to find. Label the area where you would expect to find the strongest winds.*

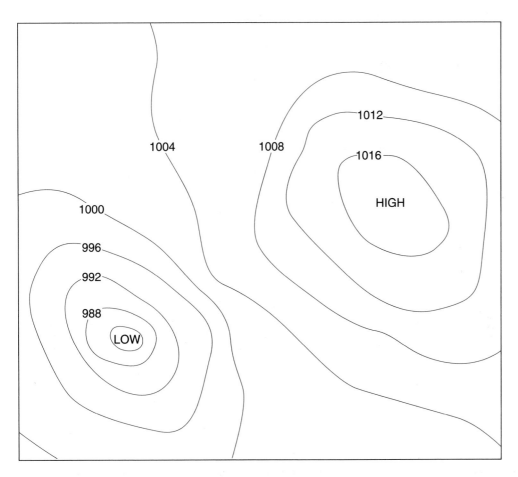

REMEMBER
Depressions are low pressure weather systems. Anticyclones are high pressure weather systems.

Depressions – low pressure

 Low pressure areas are created when air rises (see the picture, below on the right). This may occur when the air is warmer than its surroundings, or because it is forced upwards. Winds blow in towards the centre of low pressure areas. When air rises it cools and clouds form. You can easily recognise low pressure areas on weather satellite images where you see large cloud masses.

22

! **REMEMBER** Low pressure systems usually bring unstable weather conditions.

Effects on the weather

Low pressure systems usually bring unsettled, changeable weather. A **front** is an imaginary line drawn by a forecaster on a weather map to separate colder and warmer air (see the picture below on the left).

Where there is a front, warm air is forced to rise up over cold air. As the warm air rises, it cools, **water vapour** condenses to form clouds and rain falls.

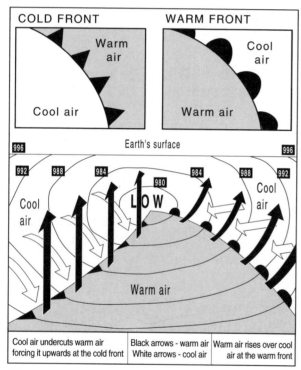

Warm and cold fronts

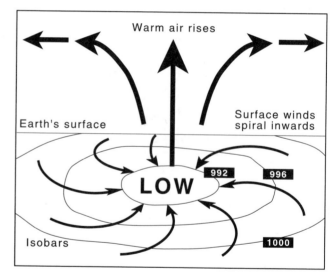

A low pressure system

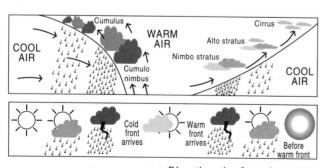

These two diagrams show the changes as a frontal system passes over

◉ *Look at the diagrams on the left showing a frontal system passing over. Write a paragraph saying how:*
1 the temperature
2 type and amount of clouds
3 the weather
changes as the system moves past.

Anticyclones – high pressure

Anticyclones are high pressure areas associated with sinking air (see the picture on the left below). They usually bring very settled and dry weather. This is because sinking air prevents smaller pockets of air from rising so few clouds form and there is little or no rain. Fog, mist and poor visibility are often associated with anticyclonic weather. Try completing this paragraph about it:

⊚ *In summer, anticyclones usually bring _____ skies. The full power of the sun can _____ the Earth's surface, giving _____weather. As pockets of air cannot _____ there is little _____ or _____ . Winds tend to be ___. There may be occasional _____. In winter, anticyclones also bring clear and ____ weather, but it is usually____. At night, the lack of ____ _____ allows heat to ____ and so temperatures ____ quickly. The ground gets cold and _____ the air in contact with it. A_____ _____ may occur if the temperature of the ground falls below _____ .*

> **REMEMBER**
> Winds blow slightly outwards from the centre of an anticyclone.

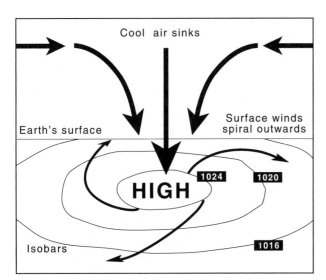

Cool air sinks

Earth's surface

Surface winds spiral outwards

HIGH   1024   1020

1016

Isobars

High pressure system

Fog and mist

Fog is simply dense cloud at ground level which gives very poor visibility. If the temperature falls low enough as air cools, condensation will occur, forming water droplets and clouds.

Mist is a 'thin' fog. Sometimes mist or fog may form along the coast when moist air from the warmer sea passes over a cold land surface and cools, resulting in condensation and the formation of low cloud.

When the temperature falls below freezing, the water droplets will freeze onto surfaces like untreated roads. This freezing fog creates dangerous driving conditions.

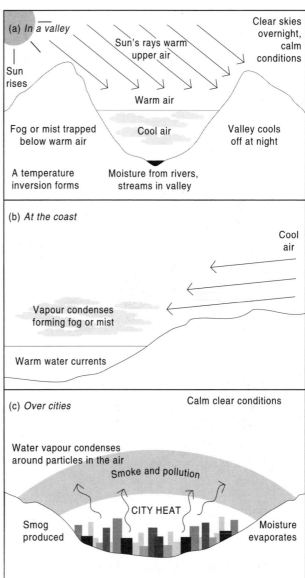

(a) *In a valley*

Clear skies overnight, calm conditions

Sun's rays warm upper air

Sun rises

Warm air

Fog or mist trapped below warm air

Cool air

Valley cools off at night

A temperature inversion forms

Moisture from rivers, streams in valley

(b) *At the coast*

Cool air

Vapour condenses forming fog or mist

Warm water currents

(c) *Over cities*

Calm clear conditions

Water vapour condenses around particles in the air

Smoke and pollution

CITY HEAT

Smog produced

Moisture evaporates

Formation of fog, mist and smog

BITESIZEgeography

Weather forecasting

The weather is important to lots of people, because it affects the way they live. For farmers, builders, lorry drivers, aircraft pilots and ships' captains, it is essential to get information about the weather before it happens. The work of finding out what the weather is going to be like is called **forecasting**.

The diagram below shows you how the information for a forecast is gathered, processed and then made known to the public.

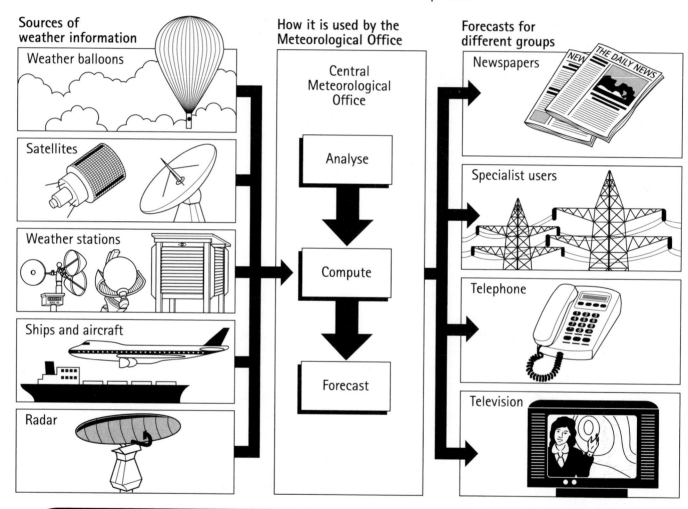

Sources of weather information
- Weather balloons
- Satellites
- Weather stations
- Ships and aircraft
- Radar

How it is used by the Meteorological Office

Central Meteorological Office
- Analyse
- Compute
- Forecast

Forecasts for different groups
- Newspapers — THE DAILY NEWS
- Specialist users
- Telephone
- Television

Practice questions

1) Using the diagram above, describe how a weather forecast is made.

2) Look at the diagram above which shows how information is collected for a forecast and then read the following statement:

'Computers have replaced humans in weather forecasting.'

Give reasons for **agreeing** and **disagreeing** with this statement.

(4 marks) ES

Weather symbols

Here are the synoptic (weather) symbols meteorolgists use to record data about the weather. A station model is a summary of the weather conditions recorded at that location. Don't worry – you won't have to learn all of these symbols for the examination. If there's a weather map in a question, most examiners include a key to show what the symbols mean.

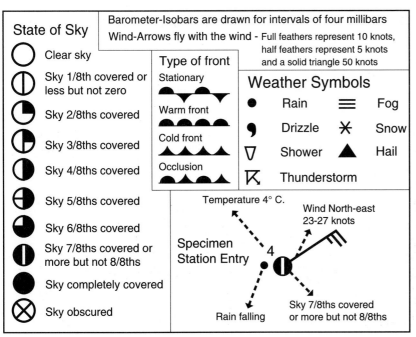

Weather map symbols

On television and in newspapers, the weather is usually shown using pictograms, like the ones below.

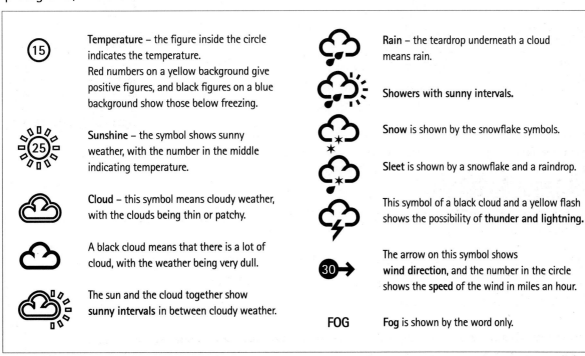

Weather maps

Reference map 10

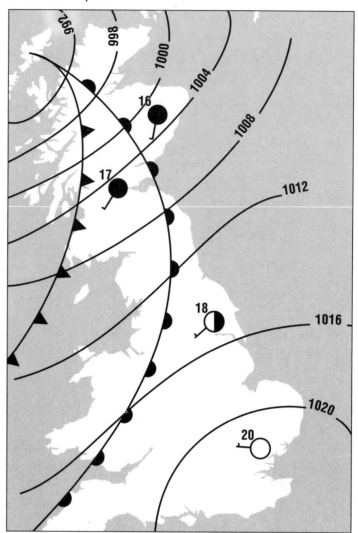

 Information about the conditions in the lower atmosphere is collected by many different instruments all over the world. **Meteorologists** use various symbols to plot this information on **synoptic charts** (weather maps) which are then used by forecasters to create the weather maps that you see in newspapers and on television.

Practice Questions

1 Read over all the information on pages 25 and 26 and answer these questions:

a) What weather is being experienced in the north east of Scotland?

b) Describe the weather in the south east of England, near London.

c) Using the table of symbols used on television and in newspapers (see page 25), draw symbols for the weather at these locations:
i) Glasgow
ii) London
iii) south west of England.

BITESIZEgeography

Exam questions

1 Study the map below and answer the questions that follow.

a) Name the fronts X and Y marked on the synoptic chart.   *(2 marks) K/U*

b) What name is given to Line A and what do these lines show on a synoptic chart?   *(2 marks) K/U*

c) Describe the weather conditions in Scotland at 1200 hours on 31st August 1991.   *(4 marks) K/U*

d) Which of the station circles on the right is mostly likely to be a summary of the weather at Aberdeen at 1200 hrs 31st August 1991? Explain your choice.   *(4 marks) ES*

e) Explain what is likely to happen to the weather in Reykjavik in the six hours after the synoptic chart was drawn.   *(4 marks) K/U*

2 Your home town has suffered from a severe gale.

You have been asked to gather information on how people have been affected by the gale.
a) What techniques would you use to gather this information?
b) Give two reasons for your choice of each technique.   *(6 marks) ES*

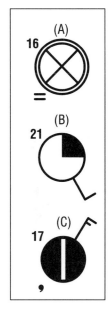

Station circles

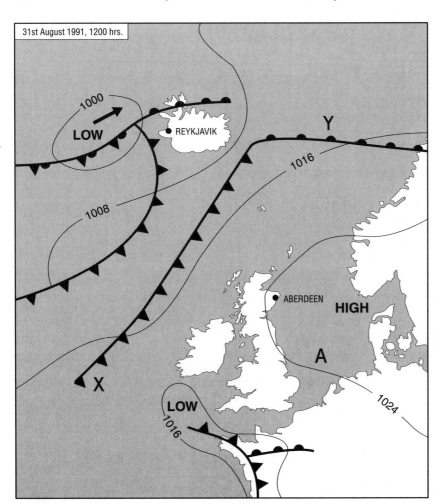

31st August 1991, 1200 hrs.

This section is about

- the characteristics and location of four climatic regions
  - equatorial
  - hot desert
  - Mediterranean
  - tundra

- how to identify the climatic regions from graphs and tables

- the effect of climate on human activity

Key words

■ **weather**   made up of many different elements and can change from day to day

■ **climate**   type of weather a place gets over time — cool and wet or warm and dry; rarely changes

■ **climatic region**   area of the world with the same climate, e.g. desert

■ **annual temperature range**   difference between the highest and lowest temperature

■ **subsistence farming**   farmers only grow enough food to feed themselves

■ **shifting cultivation**   farming an area for a short time before moving on to a new clearing

■ **nomads**   people who move from place to place with their animals in search of food and grazing

■ **drought**   when there is very little rain in the summer months

■ **irrigation**   watering the land by people in time of drought

■ **permafrost**   permanently frozen soil just below the surface of the tundra

Why are there different climates?

There are several reasons for having different climatic regions across the world:

Latitude   distance from the equator — the further north or south you are the colder it gets

Altitude (height)   the higher you are, the colder it gets

Nearness to oceans   places near an ocean are mild and wet all year; those far inland are dry and have extremes of temperature (hot summers and cold winters)

Climatic regions

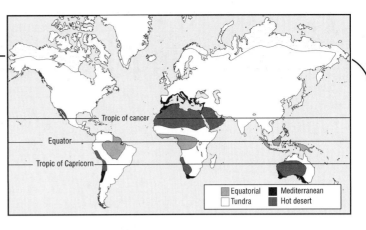

Equatorial

Temperatures are high throughout the year and are usually between 20°C and 30°C. Rainfall is heavy and occurs throughout the year.

Annual range: 2°C   Total rainfall: 2423 mm

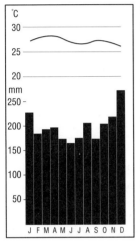

Positive
- high temperatures and rainfall encourage rapid growth
- transport easy along rivers
- forest may contain many valuable trees

Negative
- hot and wet
- soils are poor
- dense forest not easy to build through

Hot desert

Summer temperatures are very high, often greater than 35°C; in winter temperatures fall to 10-15°C. Rainfall is very low (below 250 mm) and in some places it does not rain.

Annual range: 20°C   Total rainfall: 0 mm

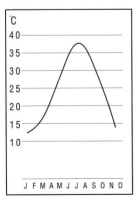

Positive
- good tourist destinations in winter
- with irrigation, possible to get three/four crops per year

Negative
- too hot and dry
- irrigation schemes expensive

Mediterranean

Summer temperatures are hot (22°C) while in winter they can fall below 10°C. Rainfall is about 500 mm and mostly falls in the winter months. Summer months have a drought.

Annual range: 16°C   Total rainfall: 457 mm

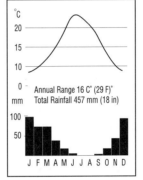

Annual Range 16 C° (29 F)°
Total Rainfall 457 mm (18 in)

Positive
- hot dry summers attract tourists
- mild wet winters
- able to grow crops during the winter

Negative
- drought conditions
- possible fires
- need to irrigate land to grow crops

Tundra

Winters are very cold and it is only during the summer months that the temperature rises above 0°C. Precipitation is low and is generally less than 250 mm.

Annual range: 31°C   Total rainfall: 152 mm

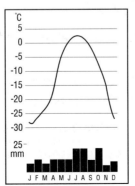

Positive
- long summer days
- wide variety of animals to hunt

Negative
- too cold to grow crops
- permafrost
- dark for up to six months a year

Describing the climate

To describe the climate of a region from a graph or table you should refer to:

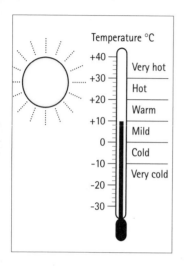

1 Temperature

Is it about the same during the year?

NO

Write down which season is the warmest and whether it is very hot, hot, warm, etc.

Write down which season is the coolest and whether it is mild, cold, etc

Work out the range of temperatures (subtract the lowest from the highest temperature)

YES

Write down the temperature and say if it is very hot, hot, warm, etc

2 Rainfall

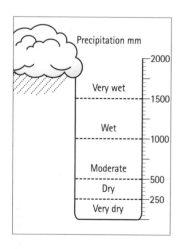

Is there rainfall all year?

Is this high or moderate?

Does rainfall only occur for a part of the year?

If so, which season has most?

Is there hardly any rainfall during the year?

1 Write down what the pattern of rainfall is during the year.

2 Work out the total rainfall for the year (annual rainfall) and write the figure down in your description.

How to draw a climate graph

A climate graph is a way of showing at a glance the **temperature** and **precipitation** (rainfall) at a place during each month of the year.

1. **Temperature** is shown on the left-hand side scale and by a line on the graph (see below).

2. **Precipitation** is shown on the right-hand side scale and by columns (or bars on the graph).

3. The months of the year (as letters) are shown along the base of the graph.

! R E M E M B E R
Use a ruler when drawing the bars for precipitation.

◎ *Complete the graph below using the figures in the table.*

Month	J	F	M	A	M	J	Jy	A	S	O	N	D
Temperature °C	26	27	29	30	29	29	27	28	27	28	27	26
Rainfall mm	250	180	210	195	180	175	220	190	220	240	240	260

Table

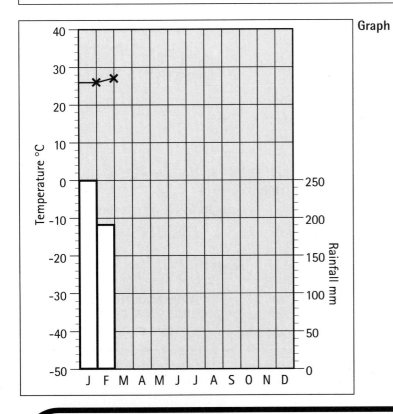

Graph

Practice questions

Using the information on page 30, 'Describing the climate':

1 Describe the climate of the graph you have just completed above.

2 Which climatic region does it match: equatorial, hot desert, Mediterranean, tundra?

📺 Desertification – Sahel

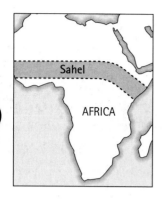

Sahel

AFRICA

Each year an area the size of Scotland turns into desert. Sometimes this is because of climatic changes. More likely, it is because of the way people mis-use the land. This making of new deserts is called **desertification**.

To the south of the Sahara Desert is a huge area called the Sahel (see map). This area normally has enough rainfall to produce grazing for nomadic herdsmen. However, the rainfall has become very unreliable and this area has suffered from severe **drought**.

The table below shows you the causes of the problems of the Sahel and the solutions.

Problems	Causes	Solutions
1 Desertification	clearing of trees for farmland and fuel	planting shelter belts
	roots no longer hold the soil together, it dries out and is easily blown away by the wind – soil erosion	acacia trees planted on sand dunes to bind soil together
2 Over-grazing	too many animals grazing on the same land or returning to grazing before vegetation has time to re-grow	using fencing to keep animals off grazing areas
	pressure of population growth means more food is needed	
3 Over-cultivation	need for food or to pay foreign debts forces shorter fallow periods and growing of cash crops	better use of crop rotation

addition of manure to soils to improve fertility |
| 4 Poor irrigation | badly managed schemes do more damage than good. Salt can build up in the soil, killing off crops | use of diesel engine to provide water from deep wells |

◎ *As a world we have the money and the technology to solve the problems outlined above. Why is it, then, that some countries are unable to tackle this issue successfully?*

Exam questions

Reference Diagram Q1: Climate graphs

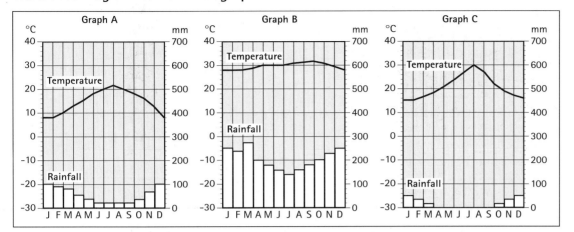

1 a) Describe in detail the climates of one of the graphs A, B, and C.

(4 marks) K/U

b) Match these climate regions to graph A, B, or C:
Hot desert   Equatorial   Mediterranean
Give reasons to support your choices.

(6 marks) K/U

REMEMBER
When describing a climatic graph to mention temperature and precipitation.

2 Look at Reference Tables Q2.

Reference Tables Q2: Tables of climatic statistics

Table A	J	F	M	A	M	J	J	A	S	O	N	D
Temperature (°C)	17	19	25	28	32	33	33	32	31	27	22	17
Rainfall (mm)	0	0	0	0	0	0	3	13	8	0	0	0

Table B	J	F	M	A	M	J	J	A	S	O	N	D
Temperature (°C)	26	26	27	27	26	25	24	24	24	25	26	26
Rainfall (mm)	66	165	254	218	432	472	257	236	490	627	269	165

Table C	J	F	M	A	M	J	J	A	S	O	N	D
Temperature (°C)	9	10	12	15	20	25	28	27	24	19	15	11
Rainfall (mm)	62	36	38	23	23	14	6	7	15	51	56	71

a) Describe in detail the climate of one of the tables A, B, or C.

(4 marks) KU

b) Match these climate regions to graph A, B, or C above.
Hot desert   Equatorial   Mediterranean.
Give reasons to support your choices.

(3 marks)

Reference Diagram Q3A: A North African landscape

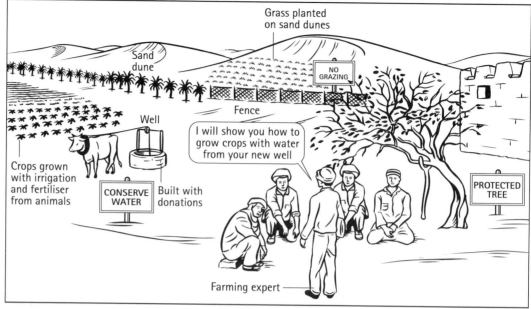

Grass planted on sand dunes

Sand dune

NO GRAZING

Fence

Well

I will show you how to grow crops with water from your new well

PROTECTED TREE

Crops grown with irrigation and fertiliser from animals

CONSERVE WATER

Built with donations

Farming expert

3 a) Reference Diagram Q3A above shows some possible methods of slowing down the spread of deserts.

Choose two of these methods and explain how they would slow down the spread of deserts.

(4 marks) K/U

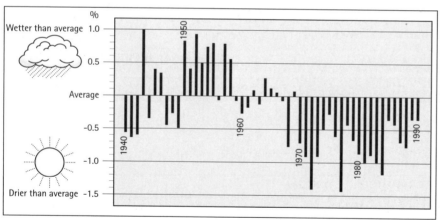

%
Wetter than average 1.0

1950

0.5

Average

1940

–0.5

1960

1970

–1.0

1980

1990

Drier than average –1.5

Annual rainfall 1940–1990 (percent above/below average)

Reference Diagram Q3B: Information about an area in the Sahel region of Africa

b) Large areas of land in the Sahel are turning to desert. Use the information in Reference Tables Q2 and information on page 32 to give possible reasons for this.

(6 marks) K/U

4 Study Reference Diagram Q4.

Describe the problems that the Tundra climate presents for the developments shown and suggest ways in which these problems can be overcome.

(4 marks) K/U

SEA

Satellite tracking station

Weather station

Oil wells

Pipeline raised above ground

Copper mine

Military base

Town

Highway

MOUNTAINS

Reference Diagram Q4: Model of land-use in North American tundra

5 Study the Reference Diagrams Q5A, Q5B, Q5C and Q5D and
answer the questions next to them.

**Reference Diagrams Q5A:
Climate graphs for Uluru National Park**

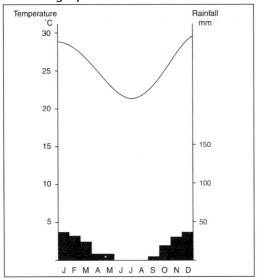

**Reference Diagram Q5B:Location of the Uluru
National Park**

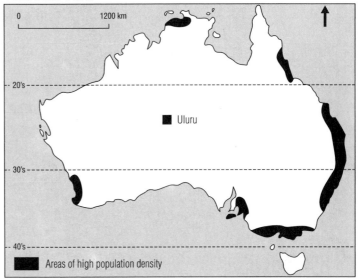

Q5C: Model of the Yulara International Tourist Resort

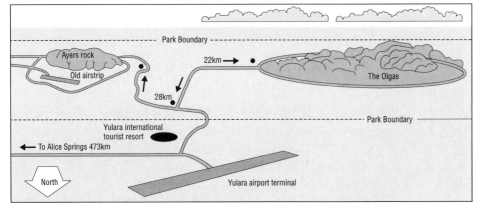

The Uluru National
Park was designated to
protect the
environment of the
area including Ayers
rock and The Olgas.

Q5D: A sketch of the area surrounding the Yulara Resort

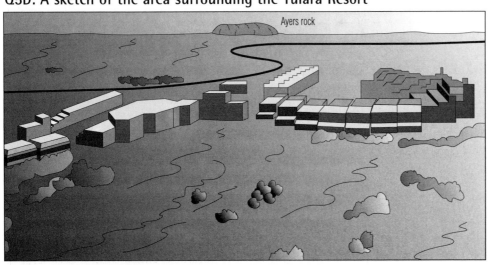

a) Describe in detail
the climate of the
Uluru National Park
area.

(4 marks) ES

b) Do you think Yulara
is an appropriate
location for an
international tourist
resort? Give detailed
reasons for your
answer.

(6 marks) ES

This section is about

- rivers and their valleys

- the processes that created the rivers' landscapes and their features

- how people use the landscapes made by rivers

(TV) Key words

■ **erosion** wearing away of the land. A river does this in four ways:

attrition - when pebbles erode by hitting off each other and the river bed as they are moved along by the river water

corrosion - wearing away of the river bank and bed by the river's load

hydraulic action - wearing away by the force of the water

chemical action - dissolving of minerals from rocks and soil

■ **volume** amount of water in the river

■ **load** soil and rocks carried by the river

■ **alluvium** fertile soil made of silt and mud left by the river

■ **transportation** movement of material. Rivers move material by:

traction - dragging load from the bed further along

suspension - light material floating in the river water

solution - material dissolving in the water.

■ **deposition** - dropping material. A river deposits its load because:

- it slows down and can no longer carry so much material

- it enters a lake

- it enters the sea

Enquiry skills

Topic	Gathering technique	Processing technique
River speed	Measuring	Tabulating Drawing graphs (line)
River width	Measuring	Tabulating Drawing graphs
River depth	Measuring	Tabulating Drawing graphs
River features (waterfall, meander)	Fieldsketching Extracting information	Annotation of sketches Annotation of maps

FactZONE

In questions about rivers, you are often asked to explain how a river feature (waterfall, ox-bow lake, levee) is formed. You are also asked to use diagrams to illustrate your answer. The information and diagrams here will help you to do this.

Ox-bow lake

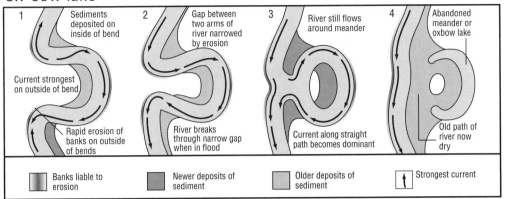

1 The river meanders across its valley. River cliffs and river beaches form.
   Over time, the bends on the meander become larger.

2 The neck of the meander narrows because of erosion. Eventually, the river
   cuts through the neck.

3 The river now takes the shortest route. Deposition occurs at the ends of the old meander.

4 Sediments build up, cutting off the meander. A horseshoe lake forms; called an ox-bow lake.

📺 Waterfall

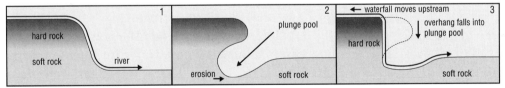

1 River flows over an area of hard and soft rock. Soft rock erodes more quickly.

2 The river undercuts the hard rock leaving an overhang. The river forms a
   plunge pool below the waterfall.

3 Over-hanging hard rock weakens and falls into the plunge pool.
   The waterfall moves upstream. The process begins again.

Levees

1 The river floods over its flood plain. It deposits a layer
   of silt and mud which makes a fertile soil called alluvium,
   which is mostly dropped next to the river bank.

2 The flood subsides, water flows more slowly and deposition
   occurs on the river bed.

3 Each time it floods, the banks (levees) and river bed build up.

4 Slowly, the river rises above its flood-plain. The levees, or
   embankments, protect the flood-plain from flooding.

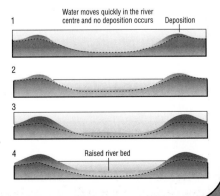

The physical environment – Rivers

River features

The course of a river is divided into three parts: upper course; middle course; lower course.

Key words

Upper course features

- **source** start of a river
- **interlocking spurs** how the valley sides fit together along the upper course
- **V-shaped valley** the shape of valleys made by rivers
- **waterfall** a steep drop in the course of a river

Middle course features

- **river cliff** steep bank on outside of meander, caused by under-cutting of the bank by water
- **river beach** shallow bank on inside of meander, caused by deposited material
- **meander** bend or loop in the river

Lower course features

- **flood plain** wide, flat valley floor
- **ox-bow lake** horseshoe-shaped lake, made by an old meander being cut off from river
- **levee** embankments beside the river
- **alluvium** fertile soil of silt and mud left by the river
- **estuary** wide mouth of a river as it reaches the sea

Uses of a river valley

Upper course
tourism	- sightseeing (valleys, waterfalls)
farming	- suitable for sheep farming
forestry	- provides a source of additional income
reservoirs	- high rainfall provides water for towns downriver
hydro-electric power	- steep slopes provide fast-flowing water

Middle course
settlement	- towns built on flat land near the river bridging-point
farming	- on flat valley floor where soils and weather are better
transport	- using flat valley floor

Lower course
settlement	- large towns or cities (though flooding can be a problem)
farming	- rich, fertile soils
transport	- the river may be deep enough for large ships
industry	- using large, flat, sites next to rivers; refineries are often built on this kind of site.

⊙ 1 *Using the lists of Key words on pages 36 and 38,*
   complete the diagram below by adding the correct labels.

Model of a river valley

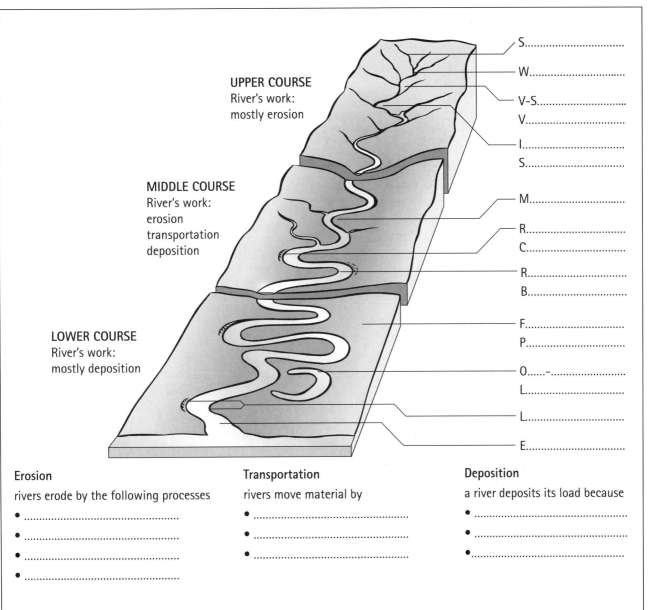

S........................

W........................

V-S........................

V........................

I........................

S........................

M........................

R........................

C........................

R........................

B........................

F........................

P........................

O......-........................

L........................

L........................

E........................

UPPER COURSE
River's work:
mostly erosion

MIDDLE COURSE
River's work:
erosion
transportation
deposition

LOWER COURSE
River's work:
mostly deposition

Erosion

rivers erode by the following processes

• ....
• ....
• ....
• ....

Transportation

rivers move material by

• ....
• ....
• ....

Deposition

a river deposits its load because

• ....
• ....
• ....

⊙ 📺 2 *Look at the diagram 'Model of a River Valley' above. Copy and*
   complete this table.

Stage of river	Valley width	Main work of river	Feature	Use
Upper		erosion		HEP
Middle	wide		meander	
Lower	very wide			

Exam questions

g **TV** **1** Study Reference Diagram Q1.
Explain how this waterfall was formed.
You may use diagrams to illustrate your answer.

(4 marks)

Reference Diagram Q1: Sketch of a waterfall

Hard rock

Soft rock

C **2** a) Using the completed Model of a River Valley
diagram on page 39 explain the changes in
erosion and deposition along the river valley.

(6 marks) K/U

Reference Table Q2A: Borthwick Water

	Upper Course	Middle Course	Lower Course
River width	1.5m	2.3m	5.6m
River depth	0.7m	0.5m	1.0m
River gradient	8°	3°	5°
Valley width	15m	100m	40m
River straightness	winding	gentle meanders	straight

Reference Map Q2B: Location of the Borthwick Water

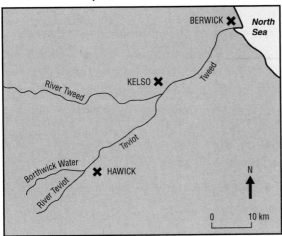

Study the diagram Model of a River Valley (page 39); Reference Table Q2A: Borthwick Water and Reference Map Q2B: Location of the Borthwick Water

C a) Compare the changes from the source to mouth along the model river, shown in the diagram on page 39, with those of the Borthwick Water, in Reference Table Q2A.

(4 marks) ES

C b) Look carefully at Reference Table Q2A:

Name the techniques that have been used to gather this information. Give reasons to support your choice of techniques.

(4 marks) ES

C c) The information gathered on the Borthwick Water has been shown as a table. Name other techniques you could use to process this information.
Give reasons for your choice of techniques.

(4 marks) ES

This section is about

- the landscapes made by ice (glaciers)

- the processes that created these landscapes

- how people use these landscapes

📺 Key words

■ **glacier**   river of ice

Ice erodes by:

plucking   ice freezes on to the rocks, then as the glacier moves, it 'plucks' out pieces to leave a rough, jagged, surface

abrasion   this happens when pieces of rock in the ice score and scrape the rock surface as the glacier moves

freezing   water enters the cracks in the rock, freezes, expands, forcing the crack to widen until, over time, the rock breaks away

■ **misfit stream**   river now flowing through a **U-shaped valley**

■ **moraine**   name for material carried by the glacier

surface moraine   material found on top of the glacier

ground moraine   material found underneath the glacier

terminal moraine   material found at the front end of the glacier

■ **U-shaped valley**   a wide, deep, straight valley eroded by a glacier

■ **hanging valley**   tributary valley high above the main valley

■ **ribbon lakes**   long, deep and narrow lakes

Enquiry skills

Topic	Gathering technique	Processing technique
Glacial features	Fieldsketching	Annotation of sketches/maps
	Extracting information from maps	Drawing of maps

📺 Corries, pyramidal peaks and valleys

In an exam you are often asked to explain how a glacial feature (corrie, pyramidal peak, U-shaped valley, terminal moraine for example) is formed. The information and diagrams that follow will help you explain and illustrate questions like these.

Corrie

1 snow collects in hollows high in the mountains
2 snow compacts to form ice
3 weight of ice causes it to move, helped by melting water underneath
4 ice has a rotational movement towards lip of hollow
5 plucking and abrasion by the ice deepens the hollow
6 steep backwall is also produced
7 after the ice has melted, a corrie loch may form

Pyramidal peak

8 three corries form around mountain top
9 Arête ridges form between the corries

Formation of a corrie/pyramidal peak

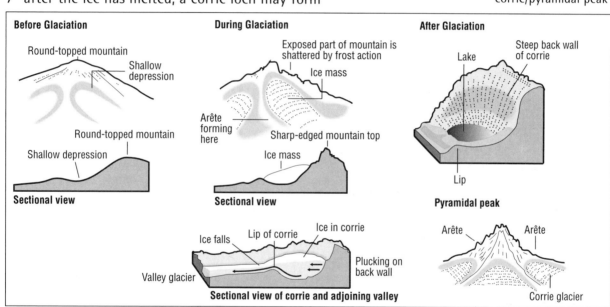

U-shaped valley

1 glacier flows down an existing V-shaped valley
2 glacier erodes sides and floor of river valley
3 the valley widens, deepens and straightens
4 after the glacier, the valley is now U-shaped
5 valley has very steep sides and wide, flat floor with a misfit stream

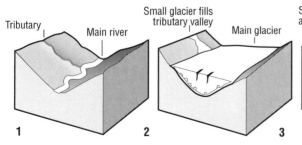

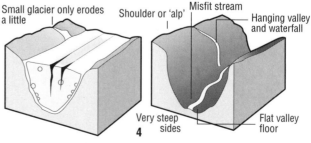

Upland features

Key words

- **corrie**   steep, 'armchair' hollow, high in the mountains

- **arête**   steep ridge between two **corries**

- **pyramidal peak**   steep, pointed mountain top with **corries** and **arêtes**

- **truncated spur**   spur with its end cut off by ice

- **scree**   rocks found at the bottom of steep slopes on the side of a **U-shaped valley**

- **erratics**   boulders moved by ice and deposited somewhere else

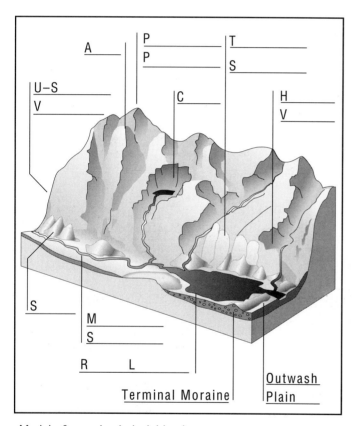

Model of an upland glacial landscape

◎ *Using the lists of Key words above and on page 42, complete the diagram on the left, Model of an upland glacial landscape.*

📺 Uses of upland glacial landscapes

- *tourism*   sightseeing, hill walking, mountaineering, rock climbing (e.g. in the Cairngorms)

- *winter sports*   ski resorts (e.g. Aviemore)

- *hydro-electric power*   heavy rainfall and corrie lochs provide storage and steep slopes provide fast-flowing water (e.g. Ben Cruachan)

- *U-shaped valley*   can be used for settlement and by roads and railways as routes through the mountains

- *fiords or sea lochs*   can be used as terminals for large oil tankers (e.g. Finnart on Loch Long)

◎ *Study the diagrams of areas of glacial erosion and deposition on page 46.*

Make two lists, one for each diagram, showing all the different ways the landscapes are used.

Lowland features

Key words

- **moraine**   name for material carried by the glacier
- **boulder clay** or **till**   soil formed under the glacier
- **outwash plain**   area of sands and gravels found beyond the terminal moraine
- **esker**   long ridges of moraine marking the path of a river under the glacier
- **drumlins**   long, rounded hill with a steeper upstream side

◎ *Using the lists of Key words on page 44 and above, complete the diagram below.*

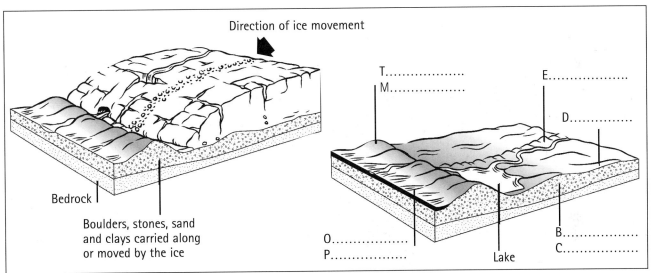

Model of a lowland glacial landscape

Terminal moraine

- found at the end of the glacier where ice is melting
- marks a point where the glacier stopped moving
- made up of loose material and rocks which are dropped as the ice melts
- builds up ridges of sand and gravel across the valley

Uses of lowland glacial landscapes

- *farming*   boulder clay is more fertile than the outwash sands and gravels
- *quarrying*   sands and gravels
- *settlement*   farms, villages and towns

! REMEMBER In an exam you are often asked to explain how a glacial feature (e.g. terminal moraine) is formed, using diagrams to illustrate your answer. The information and diagrams on this page are designed to help you explain and illustrate such questions.

The physical environment — Glaciation

Exam questions

1 Study Reference Diagrams 1A and 1B and answer the questions .

Reference Diagram 1A: An area of glacial erosion

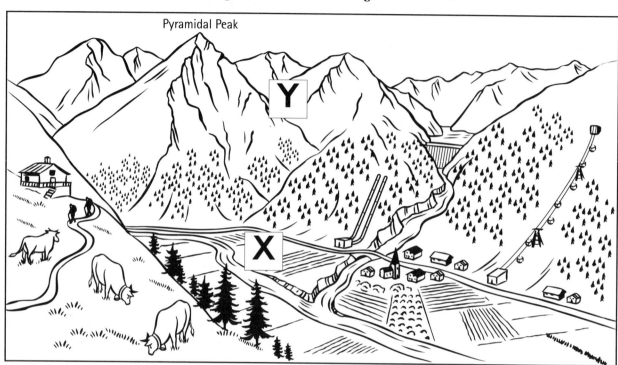

Pyramidal Peak

Y

X

Reference Diagram 1B: An area of glacial deposition

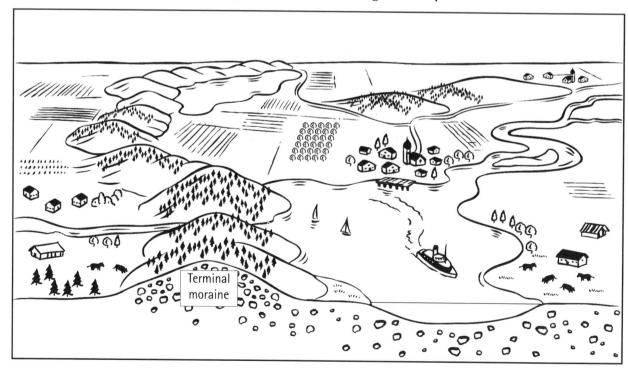

Terminal moraine

g a) There is a plan to plant trees at Area X on Reference Diagram 1A.

Name a group of people who might be against the plan and give reasons why.

(3 marks) ES

g b) A ski-lift company wants to develop Area Y on Reference Diagram 1B for skiing.

Do you agree that this is a suitable site?   YES/NO

Give reasons for your answers.

(4 marks) ES

C c) Explain how a pyramidal peak is formed.

(4 marks) K/U

C d) Give reasons why land-use differs between areas of glacial erosion and glacial deposition.

(4 marks) K/U

TV 2 Study Reference Diagram 2 and answer the questions that follow.

Reference Diagram 2: A landscape of glacial deposition

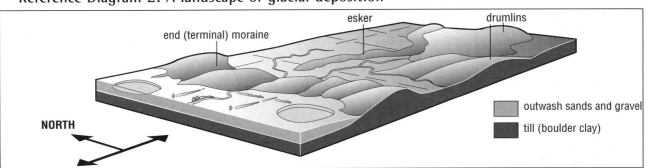

C a) In which direction was the ice flowing when it formed this landscape?

Explain your answer in detail.

(4 marks) K/U

C b) Explain how one of the features labelled in the diagram was formed.

(You may wish to illustrate your answer with a diagram.)

(4 marks) K/U

C 3 Look at Reference Diagram 1A: An area of glacial erosion.

What technique has been used to gather the information shown?
Give two reasons to justify your choice of technique.

(3 marks) ES

C 4 Look at Reference Diagram 2: A landscape of glacial deposition.

Identify the processing technique used to make the diagram.
Give reasons to justify your choice of technique.

(3 marks) ES

The human environment - Industry

This section is about

- types and location of industry

- industrial change and its effects on people

📺 Key words

- **primary industries** involve people working on the land or sea, e.g. farming, fishing

- **secondary industries** involve making things, e.g. steel, textiles

- **service industries** provide a service, e.g. banking, transport

- **raw materials** things you make goods from

- **location factors** reasons why an industry sets up in an area

- **heavy industry** uses bulky raw materials, e.g. ship-building

- **light industry** uses few raw materials, e.g. making computers

- **industrial estate** a planned area for factories, usually light industries

- **business park** area for high-tech factories

- **enterprise zone** area given special help to create employment

- **high-tech** electronics industries

- **sunrise** new, light industries

- **sunset** or 'smokestack' old, closing industries

- **footloose** not tied to an area, can easily move to a new location

- **greenfield site** previously unused land on the edge of a city

- **brownfield site** old industrial site cleared for a new factory

- **science park** area for companies involved in research and development

Enquiry skills

Topic	Gathering technique	Processing technique
Types of industry	Extracting information from maps	Tabulating, drawing graphs, maps
Location	Interview	Drawing maps
Land-use	Fieldsketching Observing and recording	Annotation of sketches and maps Drawing maps
Changes	Observing and recording Extracting information	Tabulating, drawing charts, graphs Annotation of maps
Closures	Questionnaire/interview	Tabulating, drawing graphs

FactZONE

One way of studying manufacturing industry in geography is to look at it as a **system** with the following elements:

- **inputs** (what is needed to make the goods)
- **processes** (ways of making the goods) in a factory or plant
- **outputs** (what is produced, including any waste or by-products)

The manufacturing process is seen as a system because each part of the process is linked in some way and a change in one part of this system will affect other parts of it.

> **REMEMBER**
> You need to know why industries or firms have located in particular places; why locations of these industries may change and the impact this has on people and places.

Location factors

Here are some of the things an industry requires at a new location:

- level **land**, easy to build on with room for expansion;
- **raw materials** and **components** with which to make the products;
- **capital** (money and investment) to purchase the inputs;
- nearby **labour** (workers and the skills required) to make the products;
- **power** needed by the machinery (electricity);
- **enterprise** (knowledge and management) to make decisions about what to produce, how much to produce, where to produce it, how and where to sell the products;
- **markets** to sell the products in (areas where potential customers are to be found); easy access to local, national and foreign markets;
- **transport** to bring in the inputs and to distribute the products to markets; near to good, easily-accessible roads

> **REMEMBER**
> Government policy can also influence location of industry. Incentives, such as grants, tax allowances, and low rates and rent are used to attract new industry to areas where unemployment is high due to the decline of older industries.

Industries can be classified by type - **primary, secondary, service** – and by location, as this chart shows.

Location	Features	Examples
Near raw materials	The raw materials are heavier than the end product and cost more to transport.	Iron and steel
Near markets	The product is heavier than the raw materials or components.	Cars
Footloose	Not tied to any type of location. Usually flexible, and modern industries are attracted by other incentives, such as good transport links or government grants.	Electronics

High-technology industry

Much of today's economic activity is global, with production, organisation and distribution taking place in several countries. This is often called **globalisation**. There are many large **multinational (or transnational) companies** investing in new factories in countries other than where their original base is. These very large companies are looking to reduce their costs, and therefore to increase their profits, by locating in countries where **labour costs** (wages) are lower or where there may be large markets. Many of these industries are high-technology industries - see the Lucky Goldstar information on the page opposite.

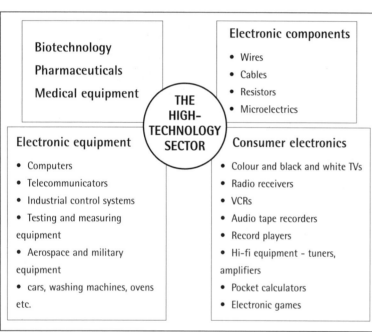

The high-technology sector

Use the information on this page to help you understand why LG decided to build new factories near Newport, South Wales (see page opposite).

This table sums up location factors in high-tech industry

About high-tech industry

As this diagram shows, the high-technology sector includes a great range of products. Although they are very different, they do share common features:

■ innovation;

■ large amounts of scientific research and development;

■ rapid technological change;

■ highly-qualified and skilled workforce;

■ also cheap labour for the assembly of products;

■ many small and technical components;

■ high value, sophisticated products

Today, these high-technology industries make a major contribution to economic output, employment, and therefore prosperity, in many countries. This is a highly competitive sector, dominated by transnational companies. Key factors in the location of these industries are: suitable locations for a headquarters for administration and research and development facilities; space to build factories for mass production and assembly of products; being near large markets and cheap labour. Government grants and incentives may also influence the decision.

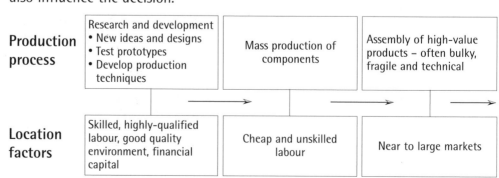

Production process	Research and development • New ideas and designs • Test prototypes • Develop production techniques	Mass production of components	Assembly of high-value products – often bulky, fragile and technical
Location factors	Skilled, highly-qualified labour, good quality environment, financial capital	Cheap and unskilled labour	Near to large markets

A Korean multinational in South Wales

South Wales has suffered from **industrial decline** - the decline of coal mining, iron and steel manufacture and heavy engineering. This resulted in high levels of unemployment and derelict land and factories. Some of the consequences of industrial decline are described on the next page. Part of the region is a Development Area which means that it can receive **financial aid** from the British government. There are **grants** and other **incentives** to attract companies, too. Some areas receive EU assistance. The **Welsh Development Agency** has also spent a lot of money improving the environment, removing the scars left by coal mining and derelict industrial land. It helps companies to set up in the region. There are also **greenfield sites** available (new land for development).

📺 Lucky Goldstar (LG)

LG is a **Korean multinational corporation** that includes specialist companies for **construction**, **engineering** and **electronics manufacture**.

LG is making its biggest ever single investment (£1.7 billion) at Newport, in South Wales. It is building two factories. The first, to produce colour picture tubes for televisions and colour display tubes for computer monitors, started production in late 1997. The second, to produce semiconductors, was to be completed by the end of 1998. Some of the benefits of LG's investment are:

■ large numbers of construction workers employed to build factories.

■ Four companies based in South Wales will supply LG with components worth £4.6 million: mouldings for PC monitors at Llantrisant; polystyrene packaging at Tonypandy; cardboard boxes at Newport; printing manuals at Pontypool.

■ Over 200 'coreworkers' to visit LG's Kumi factory in Korea for training.

■ Training and scholarships provided for young people.

■ LG Electronics Training Centre built nearby at Cwmbran to train over 600 people for the factories.

■ Links made with University of Wales - research contracts and language courses for Korean staff.

■ Vacation work for undergraduates from many universities.

◉ *Find Korea and South Wales on atlas maps. Find Newport in South Wales.*

Effects of location of new industry

LOCATION OF NEW INDUSTRY

Growth of employment and population

Improved availability of inputs

More spending on roads, factory sites, education, and other public services

More skilled workers

Development of supplying industries

Increase in funds available from local taxes, rates etc

More locally produced goods and services to meet increased demand

Increase in wealth of local community

Consequences of industrial decline

When a factory or a whole industry closes in an area, there are a number of consequences for that area and its people. The table below identifies these under three headings - **social**, **economic** and **environmental**.

REMEMBER
Use any case study you have learned to support your answer in the exam.

Social	Economic	Environmental
lower standard of living	loss of jobs	large areas of waste land
depression	local supply companies suffer	empty and derelict factories
break-up of families	increased unemployment	vandalised houses
increased levels of crime	people have less money to spend	polluted land and rivers
young people move away for jobs	closure of local services (shops)	sense of decay and depression
area becomes run down	new industries unwilling to set up	

Government assistance

REMEMBER
If you live in an area that has undergone industrial change use local examples to support your answer in the exam.

Through Development Agencies, the Government has taken on the responsibility of tackling the consequences of industrial decline. Often such areas are given special help and made into 'Enterprise Zones'.

This gives the area government aid in the form of:

- grants and loans to build factories
- low rents and rates
- ready-made factories
- assistance with wages
- training of workers
- building of new roads

The benefits of such government help are very clear :

- creation of new jobs and prosperity
- development of a greater range of employees' skills
- increase in the local population
- improved services e.g. roads, shops
- building of new houses
- modernisation of old housing areas
- clearing of old factories and spoil heaps
- cleaning of polluted areas e.g. rivers, canals
- planting of trees; creation of new parks and leisure facilities
- raised self-esteem of local people and sense of achievement

Attracting new industry to an area

Advertisements like the one shown below are sometimes included in questions about economic activities. The examiner is trying to find out what you know and understand about the **factors that influence** the **location** of industry today. 'Locate in Scotland' and 'Scottish Enterprise' put a lot of money and effort into promoting different parts of Scotland as good locations for businesses, as do other agencies around Britain.

If you get a question about the location of industry or economic activity that includes an advert like this, look for anything in the written information and any illustrations that might attract a company to the location.

◎ *Find Corby on an atlas map of England.*

◎ *Some pointers have been added to the advert. Write some notes that could go at the end of the pointers to explain why this information might attract a company to locate in Corby.*

CORBY
Nobody does it Better

BETTER COMPANY

Seven hundred and fifty new firms in ten years. Two-thirds in manufacturing. Highest proportion in UK of overseas companies. Over £1,000m private investment. Best of business company with Weetabix, Oxford University Press, Avon Cosmetics, Golden Wonder, British Steel...

BETTER LOCATION

At the live centre of England. The choice of top distributors. Thirty million people in two hours road radius. Heathrow, Birmingham, stansted in easy reach. Intercity. A1-M1 link, only strategic East-West link south of the M62, is Corby's fast track to North-South road arteries, M6, East coast Euroports.

BETTER OPPORTUNITIES

Serviced greenfield sites aplenty. Ready for development. For sale. For manufacture. For business. For services. For leisure. A million square feet of ready-to-wear premises. Brand new business parks. Four-star conference facilities. Backed by 14 years' success in helping business to relocate, set-up, prosper, expand.

BETTER LIVING

A new town of modern business, social and leisure amenities. Yet with all the traditional values of a mature hardworking community. Only a stone's throw from breathtaking English countryside. From warm brownstone villages. From comfortable pubs and hotels. From fine country houses and stately homes. Only an hour from London.

To find out why CORBY WORKS send the coupon off today

To: John Hill, Director of Industry,
Corby Industrial Development Centre,
Grosvenor House, George street, Corby, Northants NN17 1TZ

NAME

ADDRESS

Advertisement for Corby as a location for new industry

Practice questions

Choose a new development that you have studied involving manufacturing industry.

a) Name and locate the development.

b) Describe the main features of the development.

c) How has either the local population or the economy been affected by the development?

You could use the case study of Lucky Goldstar at Newport (page 51) to answer a Standard Grade question like this.

OS maps in economic questions

All Standard Grade Geography papers include one question based on an Ordnance Survey map extract. The OS map on colour page i at the back of this book shows the area around Stirling. A map like this could be used in questions about industrial location, transport routes or urban settlements. Here are some typical questions you might be asked.

◎ *Identify symbols which relate to industry on the OS key (colour pages iii and iv at the back of the book). Draw and name these symbols.*

1. Give the grid reference of an example of each type of industry from the map – **primary**, **secondary** and **service**.

2. Grid square **8093** is the site of an industrial estate.

   Describe the advantages and disadvantages of this site as the location for an industrial estate.

3. A new high-tech company is planning to locate in the area of the map.

   Using map evidence describe and explain the attractions of this area for such a company.

4. Stirling is an important tourist destination.

   Support this statement using map evidence.

You might be asked to **describe** and to **explain** (give reasons for) the location or distribution of particular land-uses on an OS map. A **sketch map** can help you to do this:

! R E M E M B E R The scale of the OS map is 1:50 000 which means that 2cm on the map represents 1km on the ground.

◎ *Quickly draw an approximate outline of the main features of the area (in this case, the coastline, river and estuary). Mark a few of the main transport routes (M9, A-roads, railway). Shade the main settlements in one colour and industrial land-use in another colour.*

Can you remember which location factors are important for industry? Here are some of them:

! R E M E M B E R Use 4-figure grid references to describe the grid squares if you are locating a large area.

- a large amount of flat land, easy to build on with room for expansion
- large amounts of water for cooling
- a good supply of power
- imported raw materials
- a local supply of coal
- good transport routes
- government aid

◎ *Add the factors above as labels to your sketch map. Write notes to help explain their importance to local industry.*

Exam questions

1 Look at Reference Diagram Q1.

a) Describe the ways in which the industrial landscape has changed between 1975 and 1995.

(3 marks) ES

b) For two of the changes given for question a), explain why the change has taken place.

(4 marks) K/U

2 Look at Reference Diagrams Q2A, Q2B and Q2C.

Which of the two sites, A or B, would be better to develop as a science park ?

Give reasons to support your answer.

(4 marks) ES

Reference Diagram Q1: Industrial land-use – 1975 and 1995

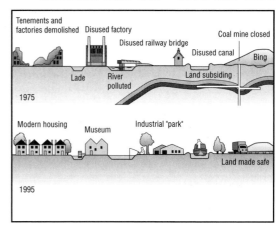

Reference Diagram Q2A: two possible sites for Camwick Science Park

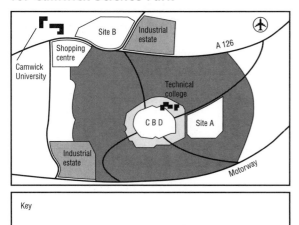

Reference Diagram Q2B: Development of a Science Park

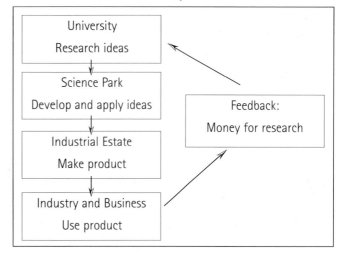

3 You are carrying out a study of two industrial areas. As part of your study you have decided to:

a) compare the types of industries in the two areas and

b) find out how workers travel to their jobs.

For each of these, give a different technique you would use to gather information.

Give reasons for each of your choices.

(6 marks) ES

Reference Diagram Q2C : Science Park

BITESIZEgeography

The human environment – Industry

The human environment - Settlement

This section is about

- the site and growth of a settlement

- the functions and the sphere of influence of a settlement

- land-use patterns in a settlement

- urban decay and regeneration

Key words

- **site**   the land a settlement is built on

- **function/services**   the things the town provides, e.g. post office, shops

- **sphere of influence**   the area served by a settlement's services

- **Green Belt**   areas of countryside around a town

- **urban decay**   inner city areas of poor housing

- **urban renewal/regeneration**   attempts to remove areas of poor housing

- **urban models**   simple diagrams showing main parts of a settlement, including:

  — **land-use zones**   areas of housing and industry in a town

  — **CBD** (Central Business District)   found in the middle of a town

  — **suburbs**   housing areas around the edge of a town

Enquiry skills

Topic	Gathering technique	Processing technique
Site	Fieldsketching Extracting information from maps	Annotation of maps, sketches Drawing maps
Growth	Extracting information from maps Observing and recording	Annotation of maps Drawing maps
Sphere of influence	Questionnaire Interviews	Tabulating Drawing graphs/maps
Land-use	Observing and recording Extracting information	Annotation of maps, sketches,
Urban change	Observing and recording Interviews	Annotation of maps, sketches, Drawing maps, graphs, tabulating
Traffic congestion	Observing and recording	Drawing graphs, maps, flow charts

FactZONE

Stirling

Basic facts

- Population: 40,000 in Stirling area

- Location: 55 km north-west of Edinburgh; 40 km north-east of Glasgow; easy access to local countryside, e.g. the Trossachs, for leisure

- Services: local government, shops, hospitals, university

Early settlers

Stirling was chosen because it provided:

- a hilltop position (good, defensive site away from marsh land near river) - **grid ref. 792942** - and other good defensive sites nearby (Blairlogie fort - **grid ref 8397**)

- access to water for drinking

- timber from nearby woods

- food: fish from the rivers (River Forth, **grid ref. 7994**) and crops (Carse of Forth, **grid ref. 7796**)

- a hilltop position (good, defensive site) – **grid ref. 792942** – and other good defensive sites nearby (Blairlogie 'fort' – **grid ref. 8397**).

Growth

By the 13th century, Stirling had grown into the most important town in Scotland because of its:

- central position; roads from across the country joined there

- site on the River Forth – ideal for transport

- position as a bridging-point across the river – scene of many battles to control Scotland

- status as a home for the Kings and Queens of Scotland and the law courts and government of Scotland.

Decline

Before the expansion of the 19th century, Stirling had declined in importance because:

- it was unsuitable for sea trade – the River Forth is shallow and meanders as it nears Stirling (**grid ref. 8194**)

- as larger ships were needed, ports further down the river took Stirling's trade

- Edinburgh became the centre of government.

The 19th century

A time of expansion:

- Growth of industry – mills, coal mines and distilleries

- Workers' housing built (**grid refs 8094, 7894, 7994**). Workers lived near the factories as there was no transport.

- Factory owners and wealthy people lived in an area near Kingspark (**grid ref. 793932**)

Stirling today

Stirling is still an important market town. Its sphere of influence can be measured by:

- the range and level of services provided by the CBD (**grid ref. 7993**)

- the links to the motorway network (**grid refs 8088** and **7795**)

- the possible siting of new industries near the motorway

- the building of a new agricultural market for farmers across Scotland (**grid ref. 782952**)

At the end of the 20th century, growth continues on the edge of Stirling, with pressure on the greenbelt land (**grid ref. 7892**). Older villages like St Ninians (**grid ref. 7991**) have been swallowed up.

Practice questions

Use the Ordnance Survey map of Stirling on colour page i at the back of this book and the information in the FactZONE to answer the following questions.

1 Give the six-figure grid reference for Stirling Castle.

2 The site of Stirling Bridge is shown as ⫴. Give the six-figure grid reference.

3 Suggest two reasons why Stirling has grown as the largest settlement on the map.

4 Using map evidence, describe the advantages and disadvantages of the site of Stirling.

5 Stirling is a market town. Look at the model on the left. Using map evidence, state:

   a) what similarities Stirling has to the model;

   b) what differences Stirling has to the model.

6 What evidence is there that the square on the map at **grid ref. 7993** is the CBD of Stirling?

7 Give map evidence that suggests Stirling town centre suffers from traffic congestion. How have planners tried to solve the problem?

8 Describe the differences between the two urban areas of Riverside (**grid ref. 8094**) and Tobrex (**grid ref. 7892**)

9 Three sites have been selected for the building of a new housing estate.

Kingspark	**785934**
Queenshaugh	**803948**
Braehead	**808923**

Which site would be the most suitable for new housing?

Give reasons to support your choice.

10 Give reasons why people who work in Stirling may live in Bridge of Allan.

11 Other than work, why would people travel from Bridge of Allan to Stirling?

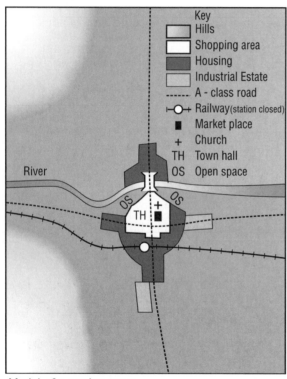

Key
▢	Hills
▢	Shopping area
▢	Housing
▢	Industrial Estate
------	A - class road
⊢○⊣	Railway (station closed)
■	Market place
+	Church
TH	Town hall
OS	Open space

Model of a market town

◎ *Choose a town in your local area and collect information about its history as a settlement.*

Urban land-uses

All towns can be divided into different land-use zones according to the use of the buildings in each zone. The diagram below shows these zones, moving from the centre of the settlement of the edge.

The land-use zones are found in similar places in most towns.

REMEMBER In exam questions you can be asked to compare land-use zones.

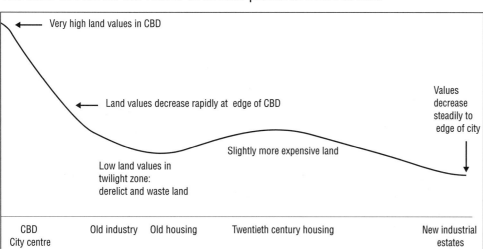

Very high land values in CBD

Land values decrease rapidly at edge of CBD

Values decrease steadily to edge of city

Slightly more expensive land

Low land values in twilight zone: derelict and waste land

| CBD City centre | Old industry | Old housing | Twentieth century housing | New industrial estates |

Urban transect

The information below will help you to decide from a diagram or map which zone is which.

◎ *Match descriptions 1 - 5 below to the land-use zones in the diagram above. Write a short paragraph about each landscape.*

Description 1 tenements, densely packed, grid-iron pattern, factories nearby, few gardens, main roads pass through area, some modern high flats, due to re-development.

Description 2 modern industrial estates, found on edge of city with trees and grass, near main roads, space for lorries, away from housing, room for expansion.

Description 3 town centre, meeting point of roads, offices, shops, Town Hall, stations, heavy traffic, narrow streets, many churches, densely packed.

Description 4 mix of different houses, flats and gardens, crescent shapes, cul-de-sacs (dead-ends), far from factories, main roads pass by areas.

Description 5 old factories with chimneys, near railways and canals, large buildings, densely packed, near workers' housing.

REMEMBER You should be able to identify land-use zones from an OS map.

Urban decay and urban renewal

The London Docklands Development Scheme is a good example of inner city urban decay and renewal.

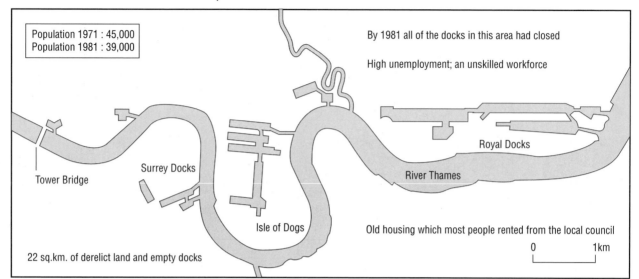

Population 1971 : 45,000
Population 1981 : 39,000

By 1981 all of the docks in this area had closed

High unemployment; an unskilled workforce

Royal Docks

Tower Bridge

Surrey Docks

River Thames

Isle of Dogs

Old housing which most people rented from the local council

0   1km

22 sq.km. of derelict land and empty docks

London Docklands 1981

London Docklands 1991

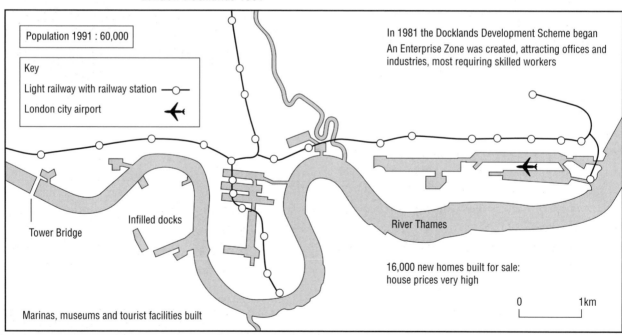

Population 1991 : 60,000

Key

Light railway with railway station

London city airport

In 1981 the Docklands Development Scheme began
An Enterprise Zone was created, attracting offices and industries, most requiring skilled workers

Infilled docks

River Thames

Tower Bridge

16,000 new homes built for sale:
house prices very high

0   1km

Marinas, museums and tourist facilities built

Using the information on the diagrams above, describe in detail the advantages and disadvantages of the Docklands Development Scheme.

Exam questions

1 Look at Reference Map Q1A and Reference Diagram Q1B.

Describe reasons why such an area needed 'urban renewal'.

(4 marks) K/U

An inner-city area in Central Scotland

Reference Map Q1A

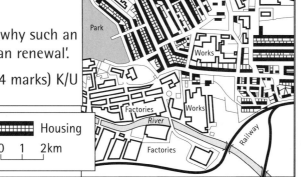

Housing

0   1   2km

Reference Diagram Q1B

Reference Diagram Q2A: The growth of Preston

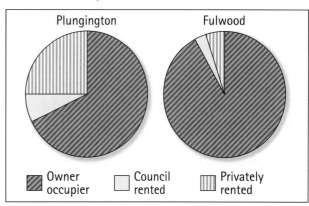

CBD

Pre 1914 urban

Post 1914 urban

Park

N

2 Refer to Reference Diagrams Q2A and Q2B.

a) Describe the differences between the residential areas of Plungington and Fulwood.

(6 marks) ES

Many villages such as Broughton have become dormitory settlements – places where people live but do not work. They travel to work in nearby towns and cities.

b) Explain the ways in which villages like Broughton have changed.

(4 marks) K/U

c) Which techniques would you use to gather information which would show that Broughton is a 'dormitory settlement'?

Justify your choice of techniques.

(6 marks) ES

Reference Diagram Q2B : Social statistics for two selected areas of Preston

(i) Ownership of houses

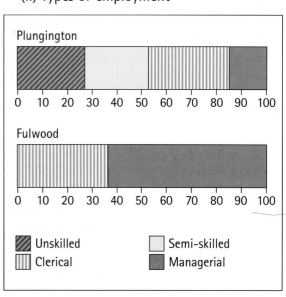

Plungington   Fulwood

Owner occupier   Council rented   Privately rented

(ii) Types of employment

Plungington

0 10 20 30 40 50 60 70 80 90 100

Fulwood

0 10 20 30 40 50 60 70 80 90 100

Unskilled   Semi-skilled

Clerical   Managerial

The human environment - Farming

This section is about

- the comparison between two farms

- the effect of the European Union (EU)

- changes in farming

📺 Key words

- **arable**   land used for crop growing

- **livestock/pastoral**   rearing animals

- **mixed farming**   farms producing both crops and animals

- **inputs**   anything that goes into growing crops or rearing animals

- **output**   the produce from a farm

- **cash crop**   crops sold for cash

- **fodder crop**   crops grown to feed animals

- **agri-business**   running a farm as a business

- **crop rotation**   moving crops from field to field each year

- **EU**   European Union

- **CAP**   Common Agricultural Policy

- **quotas**   limits on what can be produced

- **subsidies**   money to help farmers

- **set-aside land**   land left out of farming to reduce surpluses (too much of one crop)

Enquiry skills

Topic	Gathering technique	Processing technique
Land-use	Extracting information from maps	Drawing graphs
	Observing and recording	Drawing maps
	Fieldsketching	Annotation of graphs
Farm activities	Questionnaire/interview	Tabulating
	Extracting information from maps	Drawing maps
	Observing and recording	
Farm changes	Interview	Annotating maps, graphs,
	Extracting information from maps	
Conflicts	Extracting information from newspapers	Tabulating
	Questionnaire/interviews	Drawing graphs

📺 Lundavra – upland farm

Soils

This area has been intensively glaciated. The higher slopes are craggy with thin, infertile soils supporting rough hill pasture. The lower slopes and hollows are often covered with water-logged peat. Less than six hectares of the farm may be classified as arable.

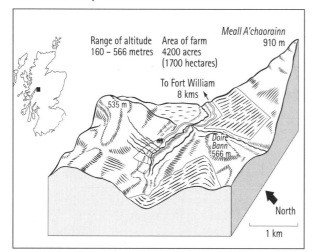

Range of altitude 160 – 566 metres
Area of farm 4200 acres (1700 hectares)
Meall A'chaorainn 910 m
To Fort William 8 kms
535 m
Doire Bann 566 m
North
1 km

Resulting income

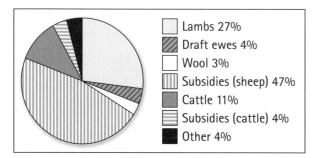

- Lambs 27%
- Draft ewes 4%
- Wool 3%
- Subsidies (sheep) 47%
- Cattle 11%
- Subsidies (cattle) 4%
- Other 4%

Temperature: monthly mean

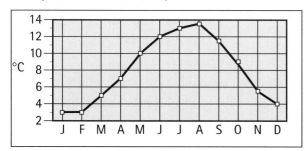

°C   J F M A M J J A S O N D

📺 Ratho Mains Farm – lowland farm

Soils

Ratho Mains has deep fertile soils based on the deep covering of glacial till left behind after the last Ice Age. The higher land to the west of the farm is caused by an igneous intrusion which results in thinner soils given over to woodland and pasture.

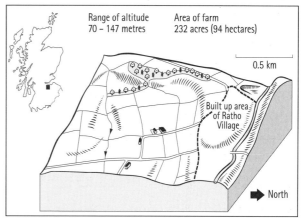

Range of altitude 70 – 147 metres
Area of farm 232 acres (94 hectares)
0.5 km
Built up area of Ratho Village
North

Resulting income

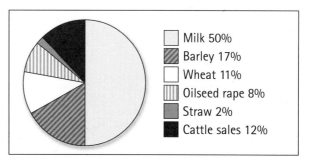

- Milk 50%
- Barley 17%
- Wheat 11%
- Oilseed rape 8%
- Straw 2%
- Cattle sales 12%

Temperature: monthly mean

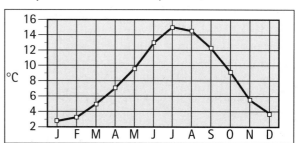

°C   J F M A M J J A S O N D

Systems diagrams (Lundavra and Ratho Mains)

INPUTS

- Climate, soil, geology, relief
- Sheep: 1500 hill ewes; 47 rams
- Cattle: 21 hill cows
- Rough hill pasture
- Grass and hay from better land
- Medicines and general health products
- Capital costs of buildings, shearing equipment, dipping pens and machinery
- Labour/insurance
- Financial support - hill livestock compensatory allowances and ewe premiums for less-favoured areas
- Transport costs
- Marketing costs
- Accounting costs

PROCESSES  OUTPUTS

- Grazing
- Shearing
- Dipping
- Mating
- Lambing
- Gathering
- Marketing
- Health care
- Maintenance

Lundavra

- Lambs provide cash from the sales in autumn
- Some female lambs or gimmers are kept to become breeding ewes
- Some ewes are sold to other farmers from breeding stock
- Cash from the sale of hill cattle
- Dung from the animals increases fertility of pastures

FEEDBACK INTO SYSTEM AS INPUTS

INPUTS

- Climate, soil, geology, relief
- Moderately fertile undulating land
- Dairy herd: 50 cows and 40 followers
- Medicines and general health products
- Seeds and fertiliser
- Capital costs of building and machinery. The largest machinery investment - a combine harvester - is shared with a neighbouring farm
- Labour - 3.8 full-time workers
- Transport costs
- Marketing costs
- Accounting costs

PROCESSES OUTPUTS

- Ploughing
- Sowing
- Spraying
- Harvesting
- Grazing
- Milking
- Silage making
- Marketing
- Health care
- Maintenance

Ratho Mains

- Milk sales. The herd was cut by 16 cows due to EC quotas but milk remains the most important source of income for Ratho Mains Farm
- Grass: 54 acres of rotation grass and 16 acres of permanent grass ensure self-sufficiency in fodder
- Arable crops such as wheat, barley and oilseed rape. An experiment with combine peas proved unsuccessful due to the crop collapsing and being too low to be harvested with ease
- Cattle sales
- A small amount of straw is baled and sold to local horse owners
- Dung from animals increases fertility of land

 FEEDBACK INTO SYSTEM AS INPUTS

Comparison of an upland farm and a lowland farm

◎ *Look carefully at the information on the two farms: Upland (Lundrava and the Lowland (Ratho Mains).*

Write a detailed description comparing the farms. Use the information in the tables, maps, diagrams and graphs in the FactZONE (page 63).

Use the main headings below.

- *Location*
- *Climate*
- *Inputs*
- *Outputs*
- *The landscape of the farm*
- *Soils*
- *Processes*
- *Access to markets.*

R E M E M B E R Diagrams can help you both to revise a topic and to explain a process in an examination answer.

65

The human environment — Farming

Practice questions

Use the Ordnance Survey map of Stirling on colour page i at the back of this book to answer the following questions.

1.

Zone	Land-use
Upland	
Lower Slopes	
Carse of Forth	

Decide which of the following farming land-uses are the most appropriate for the zones shown in the table:

sheep   cattle   crops

Now copy and complete a table like the one above. Explain the land-uses using map evidence.

2. Compare the location of Drumbrae Farm (**grid ref. 8097**) with that of Westleys Farm (**grid ref. 7796**).

Which of the two farms is more likely to be a sheep farm?

Give reasons for your choice.

3. Identify two problems, one physical and one human, that the farmer at Westleys Farm (**grid ref. 7796**) has had to overcome.

4. The area shown in the map is important for farming. However, farmland is under pressure by developers to be used for other purposes.

Using map evidence, identify some of the new uses for former farmland.

5. Match the land-uses below to the following grid references:

7897   7798   7791

Woodland   Shelter belts   Picnics/walks

6. The new market in Stirling is at **grid ref. 782952**.

Farmers come from all over Scotland to the market. What are the advantages of the site to them?

7. Why do you think Stirling market moved from the area at **grid ref. 7993** to Kildean at **grid ref. 7895**?

REMEMBER Use all the information given in a Reference Diagram to help you answer the question.

The aim of the CAP is:

■ to develop agriculture in Europe into a more efficient and productive industry

■ to ensure farmers get a reasonable income, e.g. guaranteed prices

■ to ensure there is enough food at a reasonable price.

The main effects of the CAP are:

■ farms have increased in size

■ hedgerows have been removed to make larger fields. This means that larger and more efficient machines can be used

■ the use of more machines has meant fewer people are needed to work on the farms

■ wildlife habitats have been lost. This is a major concern to conservationist groups, e.g. the RSPB and the Nature Conservancy Council

■ The EU is self-sufficient in many food products, especially cereals and dairy products

■ There are now surpluses of some products, e.g. milk, butter and wine. (These are referred to as 'butter mountains' and 'wine lakes'.)

■ storing these surpluses is very costly

■ the cost of the CAP is increasing sharply each year.

Steps have been taken to reduce the surpluses:

1 Quotas - limits on production, e.g. the number of litres of milk. There has been a move away from dairy farming to sheep farming.

2 Growth of other crops — farmers are encouraged to grow other crops, e.g. oil seed rape instead of wheat.

3 Use of the land for non-farming purposes — e.g. leisure and recreation.

4 Set-aside land — taking fields out of production. Farmers are paid not to grow crops.

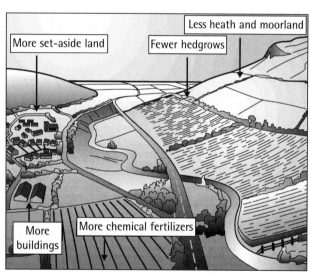

More set-aside land | Less heath and moorland | Fewer hedgrows | More buildings | More chemical fertilizers

Farm landscape changes

Look at the diagram above. It shows some of the changes in the farm landscape.
Choose two changes and explain why they have happened.
Not everyone is happy about the changes in the farming landscape.
Name a group who are not happy with these changes and explain why.

Exam questions

Reference Diagram Q1 : A Lake District farm

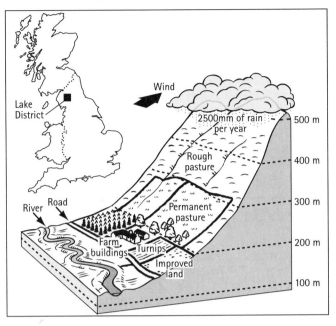

1 Look at Reference Diagram Q1 on the left.

f a) Give two reasons why the land between 200 metres and 400 metres is not used for growing crops.

(2 marks) K/U

f b) Give two reasons why the low land is used for sheep grazing in winter.

(2 marks) K/U

g 2 a) Describe the changes in UK farming shown in the graphs below.

(3 marks) ES

g b) Explain why these changes have taken place.

Reference Diagram Q2: Changes in UK farming

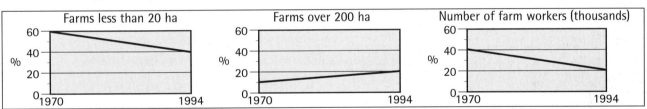

(4 marks) K/U

Reference Diagram Q3: Allan Farm in 1930 and 1995

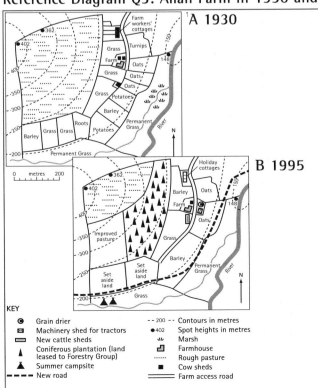

3 You are undertaking a study to show the changes in land-use on Allan Farm since 1930.

C a) Describe two techniques which you would use to gather information to show the changes in land-use.

Give reasons for your choice of each technique.

(6 marks) ES

C b) Which techniques would you use to show the relationship between land-use and relief?

Justify your choice of techniques.

(4 marks) ES

C c) Explain the changes in Allan Farm between 1930 and 1995.

(6 marks) K/U

BITESIZEgeography

This section is about

- how population is measured

- the growth and change in populations

- migration

Key words

- **population** the number of people in a country

- **census** a count of the population

- **vital registration** record of births, marriages and deaths

- **population density** measure of how crowded a country is

- **population distribution** where people live in a country

- **birth rate** number of births per 1 000 people

- **death rate** number of deaths per 1 000 people

- **natural population increase** difference between the birth and death rate

- **migration** movement of people in or out of an area

- **urbanisation** movement of people to live in a city

- **counterurbanisation** movement of more affluent people to the edge of cities

- **shanty towns** areas of squatter housing around a city in Less Economically Developed Countries (LEDCs)

Enquiry skills

Topic	Gathering technique	Processing technique
Census	Extracting information from maps Observing and recording	
Population Growth/Change	Observing and recording Questionnaire/interview Extracting information from maps Observing and recording Extracting information from newspapers Questionnaire/interviews	Classifying, tabulating Drawing graphs, maps Annotating of graphs, charts, maps
Migration	Questionnaire/interviews Extracting information from maps	

Census

A **census** asks basic questions about people, for example, their age, sex, nationality, occupation, education, the house they live in, ethnic background. In the United Kingdom we take a census every ten years. The last census was in 1991. Taking a census is not an easy exercise and many countries face a number of problems in carrying out a census.

◎ *Using the diagram below for information, make a list of the problems in carrying out a census in Bolivia.*

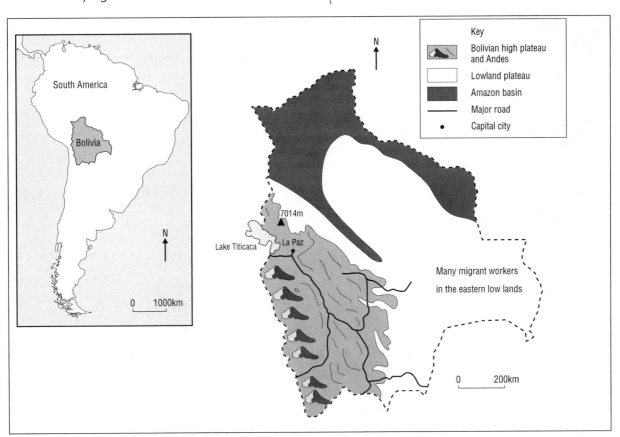

Key
- Bolivian high plateau and Andes
- Lowland plateau
- Amazon basin
- Major road
- Capital city

South America

Bolivia

0   1000km

N

7014m

Lake Titicaca   La Paz

Many migrant workers in the eastern low lands

0   200km

Despite these problems, many countries like Bolivia still carry out a census for the following reasons:

- to find out the size of the population

- to measure changes in the population

- to gather information and direct money and resources to the areas of greatest need, e.g. young or old. LEDCs need to ensure the best possible use of the limited resources they have

- to plan for the future, e.g. building of new hospitals and schools

- to plan for the increase in people living on pensions, a growing problem for MEDCs (More Economically Developed Countries)

Growth and changes in population

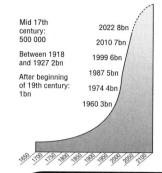

Mid 17th century: 500 000

Between 1918 and 1927 2bn

After beginning of 19th century: 1bn

2022 8bn
2010 7bn
1999 6bn
1987 5bn
1974 4bn
1960 3bn

The diagram on the left shows how the world's population has grown. The rate of growth has increased over the recent past. This rapid growth can be explained by:

- a reduction in the death rate
- improvements in health care.

It is worrying that this growth in world population has been in those parts of the world least able to cope with the problems caused by population growth, for example, in the LEDCs.

Practice questions

Showing changes in population

Population Pyramids (top right) show the age and sex make-up of a population. They can reveal changes in birth and death rates, immigration into or out of a country and such events as famines, epidemics and wars.

A Demographic Transition Model (middle and bottom right) shows how any country's population passes through a series of stages.

Describe the differences between the population structures of Japan and Bangladesh. Give reasons for the differences.

Population Pyramids for Japan and Bangladesh

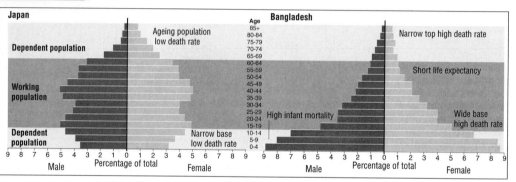

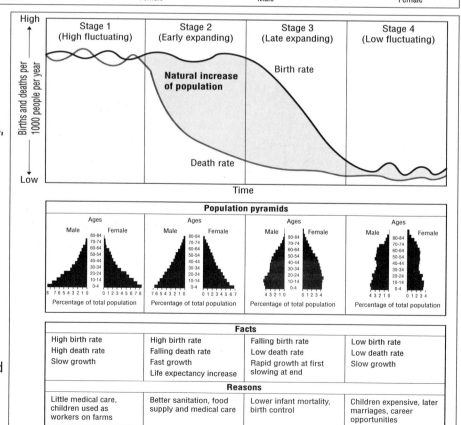

	Facts		
High birth rate	High birth rate	Falling birth rate	Low birth rate
High death rate	Falling death rate	Low death rate	Low death rate
Slow growth	Fast growth	Rapid growth at first slowing at end	Slow growth
	Life expectancy increase		

	Reasons		
Little medical care, children used as workers on farms	Better sanitation, food supply and medical care	Lower infant mortality, birth control	Children expensive, later marriages, career opportunities

 # Migration

Urbanisation - some key facts

- In 1900, only about 10% of the world's population lived in **urban areas**.

- Today, nearly 60% of the world's population live in urban areas.

- In Europe, about 75% of the population live in urban areas.

- In South East Asia, about 30% of the population live in urban areas.

- In Europe and North America, the most rapid period of urbanisation was in the 19th century, as a result of the Industrial Revolution.

- The largest movement of people to towns and cities in LEDCs has been since 1945.

Urbanisation in LEDCs

Rural-urban migration is one of the main reasons for the rapid growth of cities in LEDCs. Another important reason is the high rate of **natural increase** (birth rate higher than death rate). Birth rates are high because many of the migrants are of child-bearing age.

In LEDCs, there is often not enough housing. When migrants first arrive in a city, many of them live in **shanty towns** - illegal settlements built on unused land on the edge of or within the city. The quality of life here is often very poor as there are no clean water supplies, sewerage systems and other basic services.

Million cities

Million cities are cities of over one million people. In 1800, London was the only million city in the world. By 1900, there were only 11 of them. Today, there are over 200. Most of the early million cities were in Europe and North America. The growth of these cities is now most rapid in some of the LEDCs.

Towns and cities grow outwards and spread into the countryside (**urban sprawl**). This growth often occurs along major roads and railways, and outlying villages and towns become **suburbs** of the city. Suburbanisation can lead to towns and cities growing into each other, making a **conurbation**. This is how London has grown in the last 150 years.

> **REMEMBER**
> The growth of towns and cities is called **urbanisation**.

> **REMEMBER**
> The movement of people from country to towns and cities is called **rural-urban migration** and is one of the main reasons for the growth of towns and cities.

International issues
– Population

Rio de Janeiro – city of contrasts

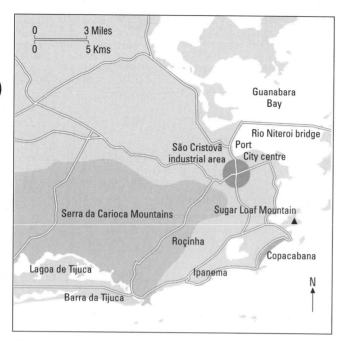

Rio de Janeiro

- Rio was the capital of Brazil from 1763 to 1960.

- It has a humid climate with moderately hot summers and mild winters.

- The population of Rio in 1991 was 5.3 million.

- Areas of poor quality housing in Rio (slums or squatter settlements) are known as **favelas**.

- In 1991 over 25% of Rio's population lived in its 575 favelas.

- The richest 20% of Rio's population live in high-rise apartments in expensive areas of the city like Ipanema and Copacabana.

- Roçinha is the largest favela with an estimated population of 100 000.

Rio de Janeiro has grown rapidly in the last 50 years. However, the rate of growth of the city now appears to be slowing down. There is even evidence of **counterurbanisation** taking place, with some more affluent people moving out to new 'edge cities' like Barra da Tijuca.

! REMEMBER The richest people live in expensive areas of the city like the 'Zona Sul' (south zone) but more than a quarter of the city's population live in favelas.

Many of the favelas in Rio have been built on steep hillsides or on the flat land near the major highways and industrial areas. When the city was growing rapidly, there was not enough low-cost housing for the migrants arriving from the countryside. Most of these migrants could only get low-paid jobs, so building small houses from scrap materials in these favelas was their only option.

The quality of life in most favelas is poor, often with no supplies of clean water, no proper sewerage system or medical facilities. However, many of the people living in the favelas have been there for 15-20 years. They have worked hard to improve their quality of life by building more permanent homes and by bringing basic services such as water supplies, sewerage systems and electricity into these areas.

In the past, the authorities often tried to knock down the favelas and move the squatters out by force. However, this did not solve the problem of where to house the poorest people. The authorities have started to realise that the squatters can do a great deal to improve their quality of life through **self-help schemes**, particularly if they are helped to install basic services. But it can still take families several years to bring their quality of life up to what we might consider an acceptable level.

FactZONE

Push and pull factors can be used to describe the reasons why people move home. Here are some of the common reasons why people in Less Economically Developed Countries decide to leave the country and move to towns and cities:

PUSH FACTORS *encouraging people to leave rural areas*	PULL FACTORS *attracting people to urban areas*
Unemployment	More job opportunities
Low wages	Higher wages
Unprofitable farming	Chances to improve your standard of living
Lack of alternative sources of income	Better schools and hospitals
The need for the land to support a growing population (population pressure)	Better housing and basic services (water, sewerage, electricity)
Lack of social amenities and leisure activities	Opportunities for a better social and cultural life
Lack of educational opportunities	Availability of TV, radio and newspapers
Poor health services	

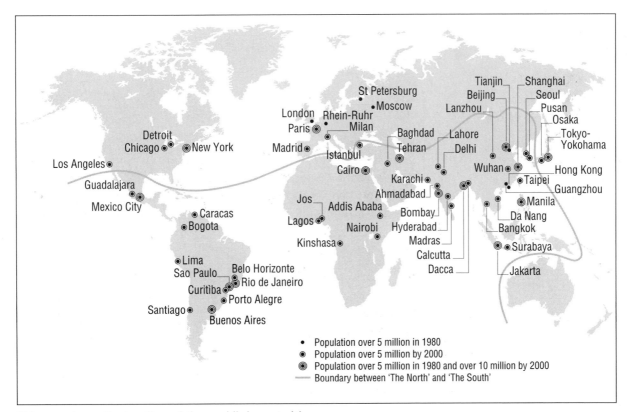

- • Population over 5 million in 1980
- ◉ Population over 5 million by 2000
- ◎ Population over 5 million in 1980 and over 10 million by 2000
- —— Boundary between 'The North' and 'The South'

This map shows the location of the world's largest cities

Reference Diagram 1A
Population Density in Japan

74

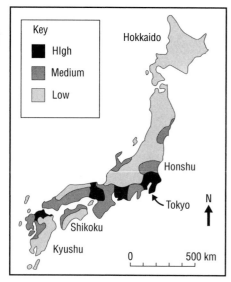

1 a) Look at Reference Diagrams Q1A and Q1B. Japan has been called 'The Crowded Islands'.

Give one reason for agreeing with this description and one reason for disagreeing with the description.

(4 marks) ES

b) Describe the problems of over-crowding in a developed world city like Tokyo.

(4 marks) K/U

2 For many years, people have migrated from the north east of Brazil and settled in São Paulo.

Look at Reference Diagram Q2.

Do you think the migrants to São Paulo are satisfied with their new life? **YES** or **NO**

Give reasons for your choice.

Reference Diagram 1B:
Areas of high land in Japan

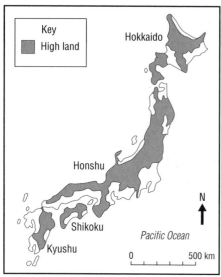

Reference Diagram Q2: Migrants' view of life in São Paulo

(4 marks) ES

3 Study reference Diagram Q3A .

G a) Describe the changing relationship between birth rates/death rates
and natural increase in population as shown in Reference
Diagram Q3A.

(4 marks) ES

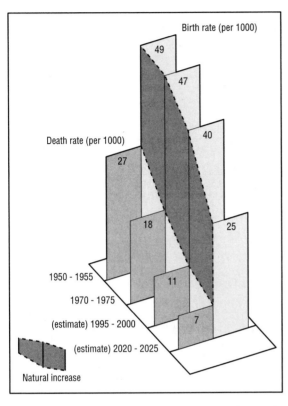

**Reference Diagram Q3A:
Changes in birth rates and
death rates in Africa 1950 –
2025**

**Reference Diagram Q3B: Factors influencing birth rates in developing
countries**

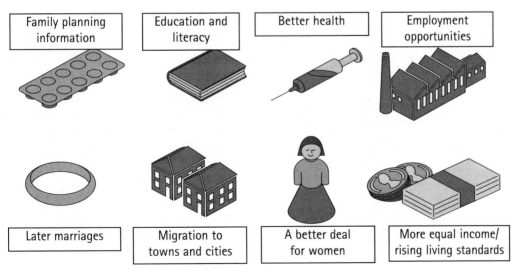

| Family planning information | Education and literacy | Better health | Employment opportunities |
| Later marriages | Migration to towns and cities | A better deal for women | More equal income/ rising living standards |

Study Reference Diagram Q3B.

G b) Choose two of the factors shown and explain, in detail, how each
can reduce birth rates in developing countries.

(4 marks) K/U

This section is about

- the development of the rainforest

- international trade

- international aid

Key words

- **development** improving the standard of living in poorer countries

- **developed world** rich countries of the North — MEDCs

- **developing world** (previously called The Third World) poor countries of the South - LEDCs

- **trade** the exchange of goods between countries

- **exports** the sale of goods to other countries

- **imports** the buying of goods from other countries

- **balance of trade** the difference between exports and imports

- **aid** help given to a country to develop

- **self-help schemes** help given to a country to solve development problems by themselves

Enquiry skills

Topic	Gathering technique	Processing technique
Developments, e.g. rainforest	Extracting information from maps and satellite images, observing and recording	Classifying and tabulation Drawing graphs, maps Annotation of graphs, photos Maps and fieldsketches
Environmental issues	Questionnaire/interview Extracting information from maps Observing and recording Extracting information from newspapers Fieldsketching	
Trade	Extracting information from maps	
Aid	Extracting information from maps	

Developing the rainforest

In the 1500s the population of the Amazon area was about 5 million Indians. Since then the population has grown, especially through the arrival of migrant settlers looking to use the forest. People use the forest in various ways, such as those shown below.

Uses of the rainforest

Traditionally, people living in tropical forests have lived in a sustainable way with the ecosystem. They used the plants and animals for food, shelter and clothing but didn't affect the forest ecosystem as a whole. They hunted animals and planted crops and practised shifting cultivation, which means that after growing crops in one place for several years they move on to a new area when the soil becomes less fertile and their crop yields lower. This allows the forest to grow back again. During this century, hundreds of these traditional, subsistence farmers, who grow most of their food for their family to eat, rather than to sell, were moved off the land as new settlers moved in.

- Over 20 million subsistence farmers in Brazil have no land.

- They form 53% of Brazil's population, but own less than 3% of the land.

- They are responsible for around 20% of the deforestation; ranchers are responsible for more than this.

Modern farming

Many peasant farmers from the north east of Brazil have been encouraged to clear land in the tropical forest for farming. Over 10 million hectares of forest have been cleared for large cattle ranches by wealthy businesses.

Timber logging

- Some of the world's most expensive wood comes from trees such as ebony and mahogany which grow in the tropical forests.

- These trees take hundreds of years to grow and are very large.

- To fell them and get them out of the forest means many other trees have to be felled too.

- Most of the rainforest destruction in West Africa and South East Asia is due to timber logging.

! REMEMBER
The rainforest affects how people there make a living and affects their way of life, but these people also affect the forest ecosystem through their economic activities.

77

◎ Find out more about the different climates of the world. Read pages 28-32 of this book and look at atlases.

International issues – Development

Timber logging operation

Mining

In Brazil's Amazonia region, huge reserves of minerals such as gold, iron ore and copper have been found. These are used in industries throughout the world. To get at these minerals vast stretches of the forest must be burnt or cut down. The Carajas project (see page 80-81) is a good example of a large industrial development within the Amazon.

Land is cleared for these reasons:

■ to make space for mine buildings;

■ to build accommodation for the workers;

■ for building roads or railways to get goods in and the minerals out;

■ to construct associated industries such as a hydro-electric power plant to provide electricity;

■ for dams which make lakes to provide the force of water to produce electricity - these lakes flood huge areas of forest.

Tourism

Cheaper air flights and the desire to visit more exciting places means that spending a holiday in a tropical forest is becoming a reality for more and more people. Whether facilities for tourists will destroy more of the rainforest will depend on the way governments handle the increase in tourism.

REMEMBER Deforestation is not new. Europe was once heavily forested, but the forests were gradually removed to make way for farmland and settlements.

The future

Some scientists claim that nearly half the natural forest has already been lost, with an area the size of Wales disappearing every year. Others argue that this is only true in a few areas and that, overall, more forest is being planted than cut down.

Some experts believe that these vast areas of trees produce much of the world's essential oxygen (in a process called photosynthesis) and that cutting down trees is affecting the world's climate. Others argue that because of bacterial action in the rainforest soils, more carbon dioxide is produced than oxygen.

One fact that is agreed is that if the forests are destroyed, as many as a quarter of a million plant species could become extinct. This matters to people because around a quarter of our medicines have come from substances found in tropical plants.

Development: the pros and cons

There are both positive and negative aspects of any developments. Exam questions often ask you to describe these. The table below shows some of the main good and bad points.

Good	Bad
Development of a country's natural resources	Destruction of the natural environment Loss of natural habitat for animals
Provision of employment and development of work skills	Local people are forced to move
Increase in trade generates money	Dependency on price of exports
Investment of money by other countries	Build up of foreign debts
Creation of power dams	Flooding of farmland
Building of new roads, hospitals, schools	Pollution of land and rivers

Practice questions

Reference Diagram 1A : Rainforest landscape before deforestation

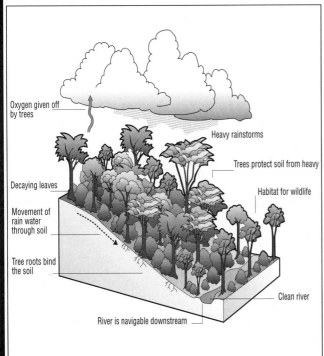

Reference Diagram 1B : Rainforest landscape after deforestation

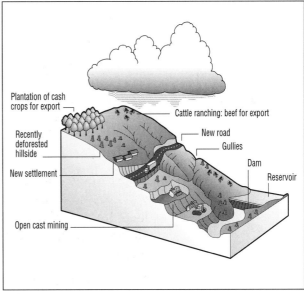

2 Despite the obvious environmental problems, why do many developing countries continue to cut down the rainforest?

1 Explain the problems which are likely to result from the destruction of the rainforest.

3 Look at the illustrations above. Describe the differences in the rainforest landscape after deforestation.

International issues – Development

The Greater Carajas Project

Many minerals have been found in the rocks beneath Amazonia and modern technology has the capability to extract them and transport them to the coastal cities. The Carajas Project (see the FactZONE on the right) is a good case study, which could be used to answer questions like these:

1) Give one reason why destruction of the tropical forest takes place.

2) Give an example of a primary industry in a Less Economically Developed Country (LEDC).

3) What are the views of different groups about an environmental issue?

You should be as specific as possible and mention two or three ways in detail or many ways in less detail. Both types of answer are acceptable.

◎ *Use the information from the FactZONE on the right to label the following on the map below:*

location of the iron ore mine; the hydroelectric plant; the rail link to the coast; the port where iron ore is exported.

Map of Carajas region

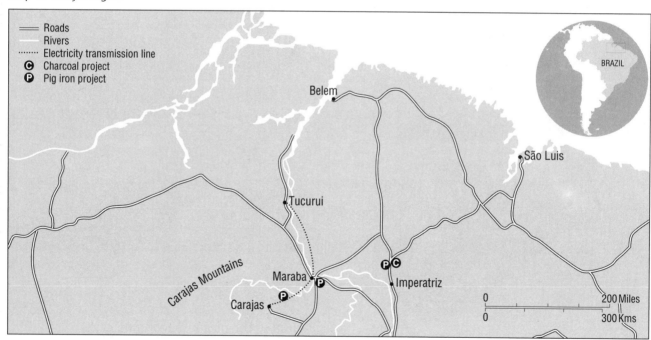

The Carajas Project (started in 1985) is one of the largest mineral projects in the world. Here are some facts about it:

■ Over 50% of the Project is rainforest.

■ Estimates of how much rainforest has had to be cleared vary, but the highest estimate that 10% has been lost.

■ The area covered by the scheme is bigger than Britain and France put together.

■ 8 million people live within the Carajas scheme.

■ Over 20 000 people were evacuated from their homes in order to build the aluminium smelter and 30 000 people lost their homes when the lake used for hydroelectric power production was flooded.

■ £8.5 billion worth of exports are produced every year from the Carajas scheme. Brazil is now the world's largest iron ore producer and exporter. The iron ore will last for at least 500 years. Copper, manganese, gold and nickel are also being extracted as part of the scheme.

■ Iron ore is exported from São Luis on the coast.

■ There is a large hydroelectric power (HEP) station at Tucurui

■ A railway links Maraba and São Luis.

■ Iron ore is mined in Carajas.

 REMEMBER You don't have to remember all the exact figures in a case study. You should know the key ideas and a few facts and figures will help.

◎ *This table summarises who gained and who lost in the Carajas Project. Complete it to create a good revision reminder.*

Winners in the Carajas Scheme		Losers in the Carajas Scheme	
Who?	Why?	Who?	Why?
Mine owners		Traditional farmers	
	Found work in the mines		Lost their homes when lake for HEP plant created
Railway workers		20 000 people evacuated	

Environmental issues

! REMEMBER
In questions dealing with environmental issues you are asked if you agree or disagree and to give reasons for your choice.

During this century people have used new and powerful technology to exploit the Earth's resources on a large scale. As transport develops, so more resources are traded and moved from country to country. Most of us enjoy our high technology lifestyle, however the processes which create it have led to pressure on the environment.

In attempts to prevent or minimise damage to the environment, a number of groups have developed. Some of these act on behalf of the government. Others are voluntary groups which receive donations from the public.

Some case studies show how the actions of some people can have a negative effect on the lives of others. In most cases the likely effect is known about in advance. Examples would be the effect of noise and dust from lorries taking coal from a new opencast mine, or the effect of banning mountain bikes from certain footpaths. However, in some cases, the effect, or the scale of the effect, is surprising.

The imaginary headlines given on the left are typical of the sorts of issues you regularly read about in the newspapers.

! REMEMBER
Learn the names of a few environmental organisations.

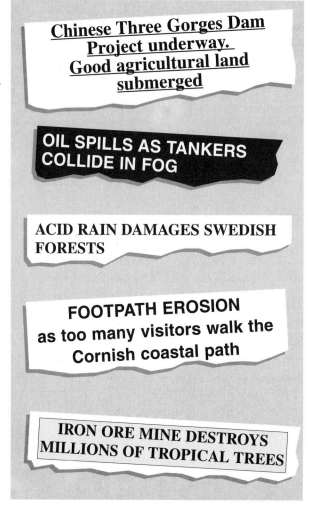

Chinese Three Gorges Dam Project underway.
Good agricultural land submerged

OIL SPILLS AS TANKERS COLLIDE IN FOG

ACID RAIN DAMAGES SWEDISH FORESTS

FOOTPATH EROSION
as too many visitors walk the Cornish coastal path

IRON ORE MINE DESTROYS MILLIONS OF TROPICAL TREES

Here are some of the best-known environmental organisations and the environmental aspects they are most concerned about.

Name of organisation	Which environmental aspects they are concerned about
Greenpeace (voluntary)	All aspects but from a sustainable and ecological point of view
National Trust (voluntary)	Historic sites and areas which are scenically beautiful or have interesting wildlife
Environment Agency (government)	Rivers, water management and pollution
World Wide Fund for Nature (voluntary)	Wildlife and their habitats
RSPB (voluntary)	Wildlife and birds in particular

Environmental organisations

There are different views about the best ways to use our limited land and resources:

■ Some people's actions are governed by political power or the wish to make money.

■ Others have strong beliefs that the environment should be available for all to use.

■ Most of us want the benefits of technology but do not want the environment damaged.

Conflicting views of different groups of people result in a great deal of time being spent trying to find a 'best' solution. Sometimes **public enquiries** are set up so that both sides of a case can be heard. Such enquiries allow all interested groups to put their viewpoints. As well as taking many months or years, this process costs tax payers a huge amount of money.

Protest groups rarely have much money to help them put their case well at a public enquiry. They become frustrated if a scheme is allowed to go ahead after a long enquiry. To make their views known they take direct action. Demonstrating, or even camping out, at the site of a new road or airport building draws attention from the media and the public. People such as anti-road protesters are often condemned as being too radical.

The links between many MEDCs (More Economically Developed Countries - rich countries) and LEDCs (Less Economically Developed Countries - poor countries) are based on trade. Trade can be described as the exchange of goods between one country and another. Many resources that we use for our industries and way of life in MEDCs come from LEDCs.

Trade links between Britain and Thailand

Share of world's exports

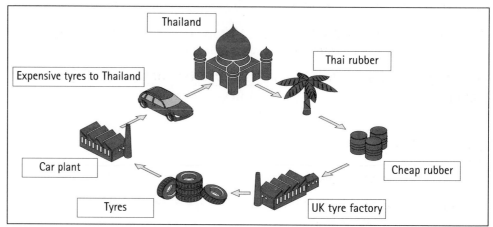

❶ REMEMBER
In exam questions you are often asked to describe and explain the pattern of imports/exports of a country or compare the differing trade patterns of two countries.

This exchange of trade is not always an equal one.

• In most cases LEDCs depend on the export of one main raw material to buy in goods they need to develop, for example, 90% of Zambia's exports are copper.

• The price of exports can change over time, for example in 1974, sugar made $1000 per ton but by 1976 it only made $200 per ton.

• Raw materials are worth less money when they are sold than manufactured goods. This means that LEDCs have to sell to us vast quantities of raw materials to make enough money to buy our manufactured goods.

• Many LEDCs end up in debt to MEDCs in order to maintain a level of development.

• Often MEDCs put up tariffs/taxes to prevent the import of cheaper manufactured goods from LEDCs.

 # Aid

About two-thirds of the world's population live in LEDCs. Most live in rural areas and depend on the land for their living. The majority are poor and lack the basic necessities of life: safe water, sanitation, education and good health care.

Aid from other countries helps to relieve poverty and promotes the development of the poorest countries in Africa, Asia and South America.

Aid is important for an LEDC's development but it has to be given along with trade and industrial investment from the MEDCs.

Developing countries pay for the greatest proportion of their development themselves.

REMEMBER You should be able to name some of the organisations that provide aid.

Types of aid

There are three main sources of aid:

• **multilateral aid** is given by international organisations like the UN and EU. This accounts for 25% of world aid.

• **bilateral aid** is given from one country to another, for example, from UK to Kenya. This makes up 66% of world aid.

• **voluntary aid** is given by charities like Oxfam, Christian Aid, SCIAF, Wateraid.

What is aid used for ?

• Social development - large projects to improve industry, power, water supply, transport;

• Agricultural and rural improvements - clean water and sewage schemes;

• Health education - rural clinics, 'barefoot doctors';

• Emergencies - drought, famine, civil wars, natural disasters;

Self-help schemes

The advantages of these are that they:

• use community resources; local people help themselves;

• help the people learn about the need for clean water and basic health care;

• involve training in new skills;

• use local resources and provide jobs.

REMEMBER You are often expected to describe a self-help scheme in detail.

International issues – Development

Self-help schemes continued

• they are low cost and low maintenance;

• improve self-esteem and self-reliance.

An example of a self-help scheme is the work undertaken by the charity Wateraid, who provide money for local people to dig new wells.

! R E M E M B E R
Aid is given as a means to develop not as a replacement.

Problems of giving aid

• Aid often doesn't reach the poor

• Aid projects often go wrong, waste money, and ignore the wishes of the local people

• Aid is often given for selfish reasons

• Aid discourages self-reliance

• Aid is not necessary for poor countries to develop

• Aid doesn't always work and in some cases can have a negative impact.

Aid failure - Brazil. The World Bank gave vast amounts of aid for Brazil to cut down the rainforest to build roads and develop the region to provide jobs and housing for poor people.

Aid success - The wiping out of smallpox by the World Health Organisation (WHO).

What makes good aid ?

• It should be targeted to reach and help the people

• Local people should be asked what the money should be spent on

• Projects should protect not destroy the environment

• Projects should be monitored and assessed

• People should be encouraged to become self-sufficient and eventually should no longer need aid.

Thinking about aid

'Give a person a fish and you provide a meal, teach a person how to fish and they are able to feed themselves.'
(Asian proverb)

'It is not enough to do good; one must do it in the right way.'

 Using the information on pages 83 and 84 write a short paragraph to explain the meaning of the two statements above.

Exam questions

Reference Table Q1 : Pattern of imports and exports for Peru by
percentage value (1987)

Imports	Percentage	Exports	Percentage
machinery	34	petrol	21
chemicals	21	copper	18
manufactured goods	18	silver	16
foodstuffs	18	other metals	12
others	9	fish	8
		other goods	8
Total value = $3002 million		Total value = $2203 million	

g 1 Look at Reference Table Q1.
Compare the pattern of imports and exports for Peru.

Reference Diagram Q2: Trade pattern of Nigeria

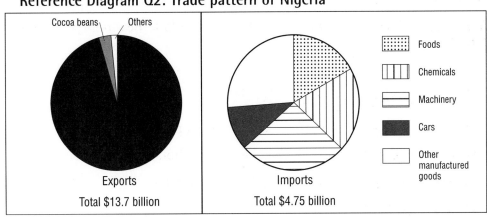

(4 marks) ES

g 2 Look at Reference Diagram Q2.
'Nigeria's trade pattern is good for the country.'
Do you agree with this statement ?   YES/NO
Give reasons for your choice.

(3 marks) ES

g 3 Describe in detail examples of three types of aid.

(4 marks) K/U

C 4 Self-help schemes are becoming increasingly important in developing
countries which are trying to improve their living standards.'

Explain the advantages of self-help schemes for developing countries.

(4 marks) K/U

This section is about

- conflicts between countries or peoples

- alliances made between countries

- the European Union (EU)

Key words

- **conflicts**   serious disagreements between people who have differing views

- **flashpoints**   places where conflicts turn into war

- **United Nations**   organisation of 159 world countries

- **alliances**   countries working together as allies, examples are the EU and NATO

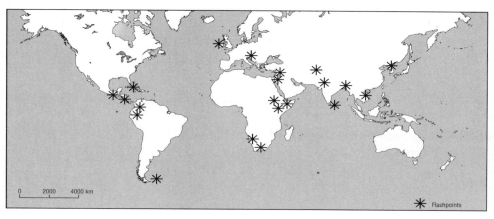

Some flashpoint areas in the world are shown in the map on the left.

Selected world flashpoints

Conflicts

Conflicts between or within countries happen all the time. If you watch the news almost any night, you will see a report of some sort of conflict. These conflicts happen for a variety of reasons. (See table below.)

Conflict over:	Country
land/boundaries	India and Pakistan
valuable resources	Kuwait and Iraq
politics	Cuba and the USA
religion	Bosnia
racial tensions	South Africa
a government being overthrown	Sierra Leone

FactZONE

The European Union (EU)

The name of this alliance has changed several times since it first began in 1958 with six countries. The EU now has fifteen members. This is likely to increase as countries in eastern Europe apply for membership.

Changing membership of the European Union (EU)

◎ *Describe the changes in EU membership between 1960 and 1996.*

Benefits of EU membership are:

Countries are:
- able to trade goods without tariffs
- part of a market of over 300 million people
- guaranteed a price for their farming produce through the Common Agricultural Policy (CAP)
- given financial support for their industries through grants
- given support for isolated areas, e.g. Scottish Highlands and Islands, Southern Italy
- given support for projects such as new roads, bridges.

Some problems

- countries like Germany are now complaining that they pay too much of the EU's budget
- free trade has led to greater competition but often at expense of local industry closures
- huge surpluses of food have been created; these cost money to store or dispose of
- money has been wasted on badly thought-out projects
- the EU loses millions each year through fraud.

Flashpoints

Often disputes become heated, causing **flashpoints**. This can lead to armed conflict between the opposing sides. The world has seen many examples of armed conflict over the years in the following areas:

- **Central America** Nicaragua, Guatemala
- **South America** Peru, Colombia, Falklands
- **Africa** Ethiopia, Sudan, Uganda, Angola
- **Europe** Bosnia, Ireland
- **Middle East** Israel, Lebanon, Iraq, Iran
- **Asia** Afghanistan, India, Pakistan, Bangladesh, Sri Lanka, Vietnam, Korea

◎ *Using an atlas, match the named countries above to the conflicts/ flashpoints shown in the map on page 88.*

Countries not directly involved in conflicts sometimes supply opposing countries with weapons and financial and political support. For many years, the USA and the former USSR supported opposing countries in this way.

Often the UN tries to stop armed conflict by:

- imposing economic sanctions (stopping trade) e.g. in Iraq
- stopping the sale of arms e.g. to Iraq and Iran
- sending in a peace-keeping force of soldiers from UN countries, e.g. to Bosnia
- sending in observers to police a ceasefire

However, the UN has no powers to force a country to do what it says.

Alliances

It is common for countries to group together in **alliances**. Often countries belong to a number of different alliances. There are three main types:

- **defence alliances** e.g. NATO (North Atlantic Treaty Organisation) – USA, Canada and most European countries
- **trade alliances** European Union
- **selling alliances** e.g. OPEC (Oil Producing and Exporting Countries) whose aim is to sell oil at the highest possible price
- **social alliances** e.g. The Commonwealth, an alliance of countries with a historical link.

Exam questions

1 Study Reference Diagram Q1.

In 1995 Austria, Sweden and Finland joined the European Union.

Explain the advantages to these countries of joining this alliance.

(4 marks) K/U

2 The south of Italy receives more assistance from the EU than the north. A north-Italian politician recently stated:

'This is most unfair. Italy is *one* country and the north should receive as much as the south'.

Do you agree with the politician? Explain your answer using the information in Reference Diagram Q2.

(6 marks) ES

Reference Diagram Q1: The location of Austria, Sweden and Finland in Europe

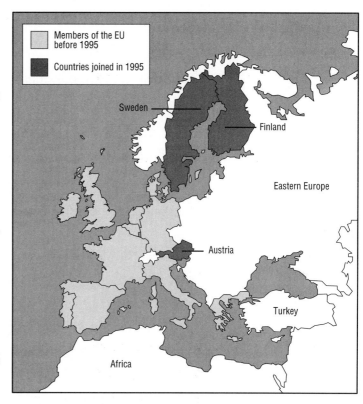

Members of the EU before 1995

Countries joined in 1995

Sweden

Finland

Eastern Europe

Austria

Turkey

Africa

Reference Diagram Q2: Italy — north and south

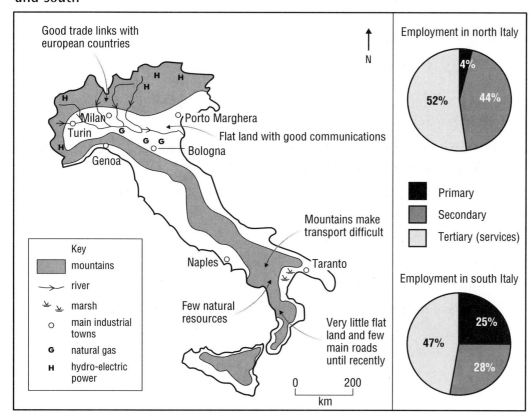

Good trade links with european countries

N

Milan
Turin
Genoa
Porto Marghera
Flat land with good communications
Bologna

Naples
Taranto

Mountains make transport difficult

Few natural resources

Very little flat land and few main roads until recently

Key
- mountains
- → river
- ⍦ ⍦ marsh
- ○ main industrial towns
- G natural gas
- H hydro-electric power

0   200
km

Employment in north Italy

4%
52%
44%

- Primary
- Secondary
- Tertiary (services)

Employment in south Italy

25%
47%
28%

BITESIZEgeography

International issues – Relations

Here are some typical OS map questions. The OS map of Fort William is on colour page ii at the back of this book.

1 How high is Cow Hill on **grid square 1173**?

2 What do the orange/brown lines on the map tell you?

3 Which of the two grid squares has the steepest slopes — **1674** or **1176**?

4 Name the mountain in **grid square 1671**. How high is the mountain?

5 What shape is the valley in **grid square 1370**?

6 What use is made of the steep sides of the valley in **grid square 1270**?

7 Name the river flowing through the valley in **grid square 1371**.

8 Name three tourist facilities to be found in Glen Nevis.

9 Why didn't they build Fort William on the low-lying ground in **grid square 1176**?

10 Describe and explain the course taken by the A82(T) towards Fort William from the south.

11 Which mill is found in **grid square 0876**?

12 Give three advantages of the site of the mill in grid square 0876.

13 Why is the pier necessary for the unloading of imported wood at the mill?

14 There are paper and pulp industries in this area. Name two others.

15 'The area shown on the map has been glaciated.'

What evidence is there to support this statement?

16 At **grid ref. 146707** there is a waterfall. Using diagrams, describe the formation of a waterfall.

To help you answer these questions look at pages 16-17, 36-39, and 45-47.

Answers

Here you will find answers to all the questions asked in this book. Answers are given in note form, telling you the important points that should be made in a good answer — you would need to write full, grammatical sentences in an exam. In some cases, where you are asked to give an opinion or a more open-ended answer, some idea of how to approach the question is given, rather than a specific 'correct' answer.

Examiners always interpret candidates' answers carefully.

The physical environment

Weather

p19 FactZONE table

Element	Instrument	Unit	Location
Temperature	thermometer	degrees Celsius	Stevenson screen
Precipitation	rain gauge	mm	sunk in to ground
Wind direction	wind vane	compass points	in open area away from buildings
Wind speed	anemometer	Km/h	10m above ground
Clouds	observation	oktas	clear view of sky
Visibility	observation	metres or kilometres	where you can see some distance
Air pressure	barometer barograph	millibars	inside
Sunshine	sunshine recorder,	hours,	in open, clear of shade

P20 Air streams

Clockwise from bottom left corner, the answers in each box are:
tropical maritime / mid-Atlantic/warm, moist air/ mild,cloudy rain;
polar maritime / Greenland-Arctic Sea/ wet and cold/cool with showers;
polar continental / central Europe and Siberia / cold in winter, hot in summer / very cold with snow in winter, hot and dry in summer;
tropical continental / North Africa / hot, dry air / hot and dry in summer.

P21

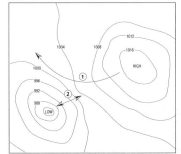

① direction of winds

② area of strongest winds (where isobars are closest)

P22 Sample paragraph: The first sign of a warm front approaching is the appearance of higher level cirrus clouds. Temperatures will be cool. As the warm front approaches, the warm air in the warm sector is forced to rise over the cooler air. The sky will become cloudier as the darker nimbostratus clouds develop a lower level leading to periods of steady, sometimes heavy, rain. Temperatures rise as the warm front passes and warmer air in the warm sector arrives. There will be some sunny spells. The cold front arrives as the cool air in the cold sector undercuts the warm air. It will become cloudy again as deep cumulonimbus clouds form, often bringing short periods of heavy rain. As the cold front passes, it will get brighter with the higher level cumulus clouds bringing some showers before the sky becomes clearer again.

P23 Missing words: clear; heat; warm; rise; cloud; rain; light; thunderstorms; dry; cold; cloud cover; escape; fall; cools; ground frost; freezing

P24 Practice questions

1) A weather forecast is produced by collecting weather information from a number of different sources - satellites, ships and aircraft as they cross the oceans, weather balloons, and from weather stations across the country. This information is processed by a computer to produce a forecast that can be published in a paper, heard on the telephone or radio, seen on TV or sent directly to specialist users like electricity-generating companies.

2 Agree - computers do most of the work / they produce the maps / process the data collected / meaning fewer people are needed.
Disagree - weather forecaster still has to prepare the final forecast / programme the computer / and still deliver the forecast on TV

P26 Practice questions

1 a) North-east Scotland: 14 degrees, drizzle, sky covered in clouds and the wind is from the south at 10 knots
  b) South-east/ London: 20 degrees, dry, clear skies, sunny, wind from west at 5 knots
  c) i)Glasgow: rain symbol
    ii) London: sunshine symbol with 20 in middle
    South-west England: cloud symbols

P27 Exam questions

1 a) X - cold front : Y - warm front
  b) line A - isobar / they show air pressure
  c) high pressure in summer so it will be warm, dry , little cloud, blue skies, sunny, and little or no wind.
  d) Station B - high pressure near Aberdeen at midday accounts for 21 degrees / sinking air means little condensation so low okta cloud cover / winds blow clockwise so you would expect it to come from the south or south east / winds are light as isobars are far apart hence 3-7 knots.
  e) Temperatures will fall as Reykjavik moves from warm sector to cold air / Heavy rainfall as cold front passes, changing to showers later.
    Cloud cover will increase as cold front passes, then decrease after it moves on.
    Air pressure will be steady in the warm sector, then decrease as cold front passes, to increase later as it has passed.

2 a) **techniques** - questionnaire / interview / photographs / video
  b) **reasons** - primary source / asking people affected / accurate and up-to-date / can compare before and after pictures

Climate

P31 Practice questions

Description of graph:

1 Temperatures are hot and fairly constant over the year with a low of 26°C in Dec/Jan and a high of 30°C in April - the range is 4 °C.
  This area has a very wet climate with rainfall occurring throughout the year. There is a total of 2560 mm.
  Less rainfall occurs when the temperature reaches its maximum between March and June.

2 It is an equatorial climate.

P32 Desertification: lack of local knowledge and resources, misuse of funds given, government corruption, wars, famine, lack of education etc.

P33 Exam questions

1 a) Graph A - temperature varies from a low of 9° in winter to a maximum of 22° in summer - range of 13°.
    It rains every month with a winter maximum and summer drought.
    Graph B - Very hot with temperature constant throughout the year at about 28 degrees. Rainfall is high and occurs throughout the year..
    Graph C - temperatures vary from a minimum of 15° in winter to a maximum of 32° in summer - range of 17°. Rainfall is very low with no rainfall in the summer months.
  b) Graph A - Mediterranean ; Graph B - Equatorial; Graph C - Hot desert

2 Table A - temperatures vary from a low of 17° in Dec/Jan to a maximum of 33° in June/July. The range of temperature is 16°. Rainfall is very low with a total of 24 mm per year falling in the months of July to September. There is a winter drought.
  Table B - temperatures are fairly constant and only vary from 24 to 27° - 3° range in temperature. Rainfall is high with a total of 3651 mm and occurs throughout the year with a summer maximum.
  Table C - temperatures range from a low of 9° in Jan to a max. of 28° in July - range of 19 °. Rainfall occurs through the year, though most falls in winter with a summer drought giving a total of 402 mm per year
  Table A - Hot desert ; Table B - Equatorial ; Table C - Mediterranean.

3 a) Irrigation - supplies water to land / binds soil together.
    Trees - shelter soil from high temperatures and prevent sand moving;

may increase rainfall.
Farming experts - give advice on best way to create barriers to moving sand / show farmers how to conserve soil / introduce new seeds.

3 b) Reasons - deforestation; over-grazing; over-cultivation; poor irrigation; the Sahel since 1970 has been drier than the normal; experienced drought / low rainfall.

4 Problems - low temperatures make it difficult to work outside; risk of frostbite. Oil can stop flowing in the low temperatures. Sea freezes in winter so whaling has to stop. The melting of the top soil in summer causes subsidence for roads and buildings. Severe weather can isolate the area in winter.
Solutions — Warm oil to keep it flowing; raise pipeline above ground to stop it melting the permafrost; build roads with a thick base of gravel to stop subsidence; cover working areas to reduce effects of the winter weather; automate the operations so people not required in winter.

5 a) description of temperatures and rainfall giving figures; processing of information, e.g, range/seasonal pattern; pattern for southern hemisphere; general statement of climatic pattern; estimate annual rainfall.

   b) YES — very warm/dry; attracts sunworshippers; airport already there; close to national park; resort outside park so no conflict with aims of national park; resort already there; basis for further development.
   NO — extreme climate; very remote; few attractions; lack of willingness for tourists to travel to interior; too close to national park; fragile environment; pollution/noise; resort is an eyesore not in character with environment; limited water supply.

Rivers

P39 Model of a river valley

1 **River features** from top to bottom - source; waterfall; v- shaped valley; interlocking spur; meander; river cliff; river beach; flood plain; ox-bow lake; levee; estuary.

2 **erosion** - attrition; corrosion; hydraulic action; chemical action
transportation - traction; suspension; solution .
deposition - slows down; enters a lake; enters the sea.

3 **upper** - narrow; erosion; waterfall; HEP
middle - wide; transportation; meander; farming
lower - very wide; deposition; ox-bow lake ; settlement.

P40 Exam questions

1 A waterfall occurs where fast-flowing water flows over hard rock with soft rock below; the soft rock wears away quicker than the hard rock; an overhang is left; the river digs a plunge pool at the base of the waterfall; the overhang is undercut; eventually it collapses into the plunge pool; the waterfall moves upstream; the process starts again.

2) **upper course** - river has more power and speed to erode the land
lower course - lower speed and gradient cause deposition to occur as river slows.
middle course - balance between erosion and deposition depending when river in flood.

3 a) River width increases seaward in the model and river.
Depth in river shallowest in middle - unlike model.
Gradient is different, increases in lower course of Borthwick Water.
Valley width and straightness vary from the model in the lower course.
Borthwick Water is a tributary of the Tweed; model shows a river from source to sea.

   b) **techniques** - measuring river speed; measuring depth and width.
reasons - provides original data; precise and accurate data; can compare the speed across the river.

   c) **techniques** - multiple line graphs
reasons - able to show change of one along the course of the river e.g. river depth; be able to compare width with depth

Glaciation

P44 Diagram: model of an upland glacial landscape - Answers
anticlockwise from outwash plain are:
hanging valley; truncated spur; corrie; pyramidal peak; arête; U-shaped valley; scree, misfit stream; ribbon lake.
Lists for diagrams: glacial erosion - farming; settlement; roads; forestry; tourism; HEP; skiing

glacial deposition - farming; settlement; roads; forestry; tourism; sailing

P45 Lowland features
Answers, clockwise from top right: esker, drumlin, boulder clay, outwash plain, terminal moraine.

P46 Exam questions

1 a) Farmers - loss of valuable, fertile farmland. Trees can be grown on slopes.

   b) YES — jobs created, tourism increased, more money spent in area, locals will be better off, area ideal for skiing - steep slopes and snow all year, over-crowding reduced on existing slopes.
   NO - new building may harm local wildlife, buildings can be unsightly and destroy scenic views, area would become crowded, increased traffic would cause more pollution.

   c) During glaciation, three or more corries develop on the mountain; plucking and frost shattering make back walls steep; corries get deeper and steeper eroding back on to each other; mountain is eventually left with three steep slopes rising to a sharp peak.

   d) Glacial erosion - tourism predominates in areas of erosion since steep slopes ideal for skiing. Corries are ideal for climbing. Forestry is best use of the steep slopes of the U-shaped valley. Flat land is limited so settlement is restricted.
   Glacial deposition - land is lower and more suitable for farming; sands and gravel can be extracted for construction; boulder clay is fertile enough to support dairy farming; drumlins are ideal for settlement.

2 a) west - outwash deposits in the west; terminal moraine runs north-south; till deposits are found under the ice whereas outwash is not; orientation of the drumlins

   b) terminal moraine - found at the end of the glacier where the ice is melting. It marks the point where the glacier has stopped moving. Made up of loose material and rocks dropped as the ice melts. Builds up ridges of sand and gravel across the valley.

3 technique - fieldsketch
reasons - is more selective than a photograph; can be used to highlight important features; can be used to compare with a photograph to show change.

4 technique - annotation of a fieldsketch
reasons - highlights the main features of the area; enhances the information; used to name and identify features

The human environment

Industry

P53 Corby: notes to labels could say:
- 750 new firms - much investment; good place to be financially:
- at centre of England - great communications
- greenfield sites and ready-built space - good for moving in straight away or building your own space;
- new town - good labour and sales places for workers to re-locate;
- coupon — attracts you to find out more from a specific person

Practice questions — be specific and give real facts and real places and details.

P54 OS maps in economic questions

1 primary - farming 7895
secondary - industrial estate 8093
service - golf course 7893; castle 7994

2 Advantages - large, flat, level site; easy to build on, near workers, good roads
Disadvantages - little room for expansion; liable to flood; congested roads costly and waste time.

3 Stirling has a central location within Scotland with easy access by motorways M9 and M80 to other parts of the country. The area has a well-educated workforce. Plenty of good sites near the motorway to locate a factory. The surrounding area is known for its beauty and it provides opportunities for relaxation and recreation.

4 Evidence of importance of tourism supported by Stirling Castle (792942); Wallace Monument (813958); Heritage Centre (797905) (Bannockburn) ; caravan and camping sites (790953 and 823968).

P55 **Exam questions**

1 a) Tenements and factories knocked down to be replaced by an industrial park; disused factory converted to museum; polluted river cleaned up; coal mining area landscaped.

b) tenements - demolished because of poor condition; industrial park could provide new jobs.
factory - closed down as heavy industry declined, so converted to museum to attract visitors; improved image of area.
canal - reopened and cleaned up as it was dangerous and unhealthy; will encourage boat trips; attract visitors
old mines - dangerous and unattractive; hazard to children; landscaping improves image.

2 Site A - near main road for easy access; plenty of land to develop; close to technical college; closer to workers so easy to get to; direct link to airport.
Site B - better access for lorries than site A; less congestion; more space on edge of town to build; less crowded than CBD; close to industrial estate; close to university for research; workers may find it easier to get to; pleasant surroundings/less polluted

3 a) To compare types of industries:
e.g **fieldwork** - allows you to see for yourself which industries are there;
taking photographs/fieldsketches — shows differences in buildings and between two areas; label sketches to show information **extracting information from maps** - see layout and work out type of industry words e.g mine or trading estate; helps to compare areas;
questionnaire - ask companies in each area about their business and then compare two areas

b) Find out how workers travel to work:
eg **questionnaire** - give details of how workers travelled.
interview - ask workers about their journey to work.
traffic survey - estimate the number of cars, buses, pedestrians at the factory gate
maps — can show ways of getting to work e.g. road; rail; car parking space; bus routes; underground

Settlement

P58 **Practice questions**

1 792942

2 797948

3 meeting place of roads; bridging-point

4 **advantages** — defence; bridging-point; easy access
disadvantages — flooding; marshland; small site

5 a) **similarities** - near river; meeting place of roads; town hall, church; railway station near CBD; bridging-point

b) **differences** - shape, absence of open space near river, motorway, castle, monuments.

6 7993 contains - town hall; churches; information centre; railway station; meeting place of A-class roads

7 **reasons** - narrow streets; lots of minor roads; densely packed
solutions - dual carriageway to east of CBD (inner ring road); motorway to take away passing traffic

8 **riverside** 8094 - near CBD; near river; curved roads: built early 20th century
Torbrex 7894 - on edge of town; near motorway; cul-de-sacs; late 20th century

9 Breahead - 808923 - large flat site; near roads. King's Park is a golf course. Queenshaugh near river and liable to flood.

10 pleasant village; less pollution; near leisure: golf course / hills, larger houses.

11 shopping; leisure; education.

P59 **Urban land uses**

Descriptions - From left to right on the diagram: 3 ; 5 ; 1 ; 4 ; 2 .

P60 **Urban decay / renewal**

Advantages - investment in area improves environment; new jobs; construction jobs; office jobs; tourist attractions; increase in population; improved roads; railways, airport: benefits for local people; new private houses.

Disadvantages - housing is expensive; local people forced out by wealthy newcomers; new jobs are mostly highly- skilled and go to

outsiders; locals still suffer from high unemployment; many tourist jobs are unskilled and low paid; Enterprise Zone takes investment from nearby areas of need; concerns about noise from airport.

P61 **Exam questions**

1 over-crowded conditions; run-down area; mix of old housing and industry; unattractive environment.

2 a) Plungington near CBD; Fulwood on the edge; Plungington has less than 75% owner-occupied housing, Fulwood has 90%; Plungington has 25% rented; Fulwood has less than 10%; Fulwood is more affluent - 60% have management jobs. Plungington has over 50% unskilled and semi-skilled; Plungington houses pre-1914 possibly terraced; Fulwood more modern.

b) many new houses built; larger village now; houses gone up; many more people; more children so more schools built; closure of small shops as people buy in large supermarkets; managerial and professional types travel by car to work.

c) **Questionnaire** - ask numbers of people where they work
Interview - ask sample of people where they work
Consult maps to see where nearby towns located; work out time/distance of travel.
Consult maps to work out functions of Broughton - absence of industry.
Traffic count (morning and night) compare cars leaving and entering.

Farming

P65 **Comparing Lundrava and Ratho Mains**

You should use the seven headings to write seven short comparative statements from the information in the diagrams, e.g.
Location - Lundrava is near Fort William while Ratho is in the east near Edinburgh.
Landscape - Lundrava is a large hilly farm of 1700 hectares while Ratho is smaller and on lower land.

Practice questions

1 **Upland** - sheep: too cold, too steep, too thin soils to grow crops
Lower slopes -cattle: warmer than upper slopes
Carse of Forth - crops; fertile soils

2 Drumbrae (8097) has steeper slopes, colder, unsuitable for crops
Westleys (7796) on flat land near river more suitable to crops.
Dumbrae is more likely to be a sheep farm.

3 **physical** - flooding from river; **human** - farm divided by motorway.

4 housing (7892); industry (8093); sewage works (8093); leisure (7893) golf course; Stirling University (8096); roads (7794); motorway M9.

5 (7897) -woodland; (7798) - shelter belts; (7791) - picnics/walks.

6 Good access to major roads; easy to transport animals quickly to and from market; buyers are attracted from all over the country; better prices.

7 Purpose-built market; room for large vehicles: expansion; avoids congestion of inner town; near to motorway.

P66 **Common Agricultural Policy**

Changes in the farmscape
- hedgerows cut down to make larger fields; so larger machinery can be used to make a bigger profit.
- more buildings to keep more animals; to store more machines
- more chemical fertilisers to grow more food and to reduce the need of fallow.
- more set-aside land to reduce surpluses and money wasted
- less heath and moorland to increase the farmland; to grow more food/ to increase profit.
group who are not happy - RSPCA - loss of hedges means loss of habitat for birds

P67 **Exam questions**

1 a) too cold; too steep; exposed to winds; shallow soils; heavy rainfall.

b) weather not so severe; more sheltered; nearer farm; easier to attend to; fodder nearby

2 a) Farms below 20 ha decreasing, from 60% to 40% ; farms over 200 ha increasing, from 10% to 20%; farm workers decreasing from 420 to 200

b) large farms more profitable; machinery replaces workers; large farms more efficient; easier to use machines in large field; large farms can afford the expense of machinery.

3 a) **techniques** - interview farmer / workers; reasons; get first-hand information on farm

techniques - taking photographs; recording on maps; fieldsketches; **reasons** - allow comparison of information

b) draw annotated cross-section to compare land-use / relief along section
Place tracing of land-use on relief map - allows comparison of both

c) Fields larger to use larger machinery and be more efficient; farmers' cottages turned into holiday homes as fewer workers needed (since more machines used); holiday homes bring in cash.
  - more storage space to keep more machines
  - woodland planted to provide shelter from westerly wind
  - rough grazing planted with trees for long-term investment
  - campsite provides income, new road improves access
  - potatoes replaced by barley as it is in demand.
  - set-aside land reduces surpluses.

International issues

Population

P69 Census
Problems - remote and inaccessible areas, e.g. mountains, forests, poor roads; illiteracy; different languages; migrant workers; expensive for a poor country

P70 Practice question
2 **differences:** Japan has higher % over 65; children make up high % of population in Bangladesh; Bangladesh population growing more quickly; Japan has large % in middle or working age groups
reasons: Japan has more old people as it has higher standard of living, better health-care; better food supply; Bangladeshi families have more children so they can work to help family income; higher risk of infant mortality; Japan has better-educated people, aware of family planning methods, hence very low growth in population. People more career and materially minded.

P74 Exam questions
1 a) **agreeing** - large areas of high density, so means large areas crowded; south of Japan crowded because of high population densities.
disagreeing - not all islands have high density; highland areas are not crowded; high densities only found on low land near coast.
  b) pollution; traffic congestion; poor housing; disease; parking problems; declining industries; unemployment; violence; crime
2 **YES** - higher standard of living; earn more money; good jobs; can send money to family; have flats; life is better than at home
NO - not enough houses; have to live in shanty town; poor sanitation; workers live in hostels; family left at home; jobs poorly paid; can't afford rents
3 a) Reduction in death rate and steady, then falling, birth rate; because of natural population increase between 1950 and 1975 and the expected decline in increase after 2000.
  b) The availability of contraceptives allows people to choose when they have children and reduces birth rates
Medical improvements cut infant mortality rates and pressure to have more children.
Better deal for women means later marriages, therefore fewer children.

Development

P79 Practice questions
1 Removal of trees means heavy rain washes soil away into rivers and pollutes the river, forming sandbanks and hindering navigation. Animal and plant species lost; mining disfigures the landscape; chemicals are washed into rivers causing pollution of fish and then people; Indians lose their homes; crops fail as soil loses fertility, so more forest cut; reduction in oxygen contributes to global warming; increase in CO_2.
2 Countries do this to provide land for people in overcrowded cities; to develop the countries' resources; to increase the standard of living; to export to pay for imports; to develop industry within the country; to pay off foreign debts
3 Loss of the forest, planting of cash crops, cattle ranching, new settlements and roads, open cast mines, erosion of the hillside forming gullies, new reservoirs and power dams.

P80 Greater Carajas Project
All the information you need is in the FactZONE on page 81. Find the place names on the map and label them - draw the railway between Maraba and São Luis.

P81 FactZONE
Words to go in spaces in table:
Mine owners: make money from one of largest mineral deposits in the world; poor/unemployed locals: found work in the mines; railway workers: found work on new railway; traditional farmers: lost land through forest clearance; 30 000 local people: lost their homes when lake for HEP plant created; 20 000 people evacuated: to build aluminium smelter

P86 Asian proverb, possible answer: better not to give people a handout but rather let them help themselves to a better future.

P87 Exam questions
1 value of imports greater than exports, so country in debt - spends more than it earns; exports mainly raw materials, e.g. minerals and metals; imports mostly finished goods which are expensive
2 YES - healthy pattern as exports greater than imports; by 8 or 9 billion dollars; it sells oil which will always be needed by foreign countries
NO - relies too heavily on oil; if price drops it will lose money; they rely on imports for essential goods.
3 **Bilateral aid** is when one country receives aid from another and there are certain conditions attached.
Multi-lateral aid is when a country receives aid from an organisation representing more than one country, e.g. UN or WHO.
Charitable aid is aid donated by a charity, e.g. Oxfam.
4 Small-scale; cheap; address specific and local needs, e.g. health-care or water supply; encourages local co-operation; develops local skills; uses local materials; controlled locally; low-level technology which is easily repaired.

International relations

P89 FactZONE - The EU
Description of changes in EU membership - More countries have joined, so membership has increased from six to fifteen; in 1960, members were in the centre of Western Europe; today, new members on edge or fringe of Europe.

P91 Exam questions
1 These countries have huge trade links with EU countries; tariffs make their goods expensive; trade will be easier and cheaper if they are members; gives them access to huge market of 350 million; they will be protected from competition from non-EU countries; they have historic links with other nations; Austria - in centre of Europe; near other members; speak German; Germany important neighbour; common interests.
2 **Agree** that it is unfair: Northern Italy has difficult, mountainous country and flat land liable to flooding; cities have problems: e.g. pollution, unemployment; any aid unlikely to be wasted; Southern Italy has huge areas of farmland.
Disagree: South needs help as it is on the edge of Europe; transport costs high and new roads needed; volcanoes bring damage to area; no great natural resources in south, unlike north; south suffers from summer drought so farming needs costly irrigation; most jobs low-paid, primary-type, while north has highly-paid, manufacturing jobs.

Fort William OS map: questions
1 287 m   2 contours tell height and shape   3 1674   4 Ben Nevis
5 U-shaped   6 forestry/ walks   7 River Nevis
8 camp and caravan site; youth hostel; parking; visitor centre; marshland; flooding   9 area is marshland and liable to flooding   10 Follows the loch-side, using only available flat land, avoiding high and steep slopes.
11 paper mill   12 large flat site, near railway, roads, access via loch, near source of timber.   13 too shallow near shore, so pier required to get access to deep water   14 aluminium works (1257500 ; distillery (126755)
15 You must give the name and grid reference of a number of glacial features shown on the map e.g. pyramidal peak - Ben Nevis 1671 U-shaped valley - Glen Nevis 1370   16 describe how a waterfall is formed (see answers to Exam questions, River section)

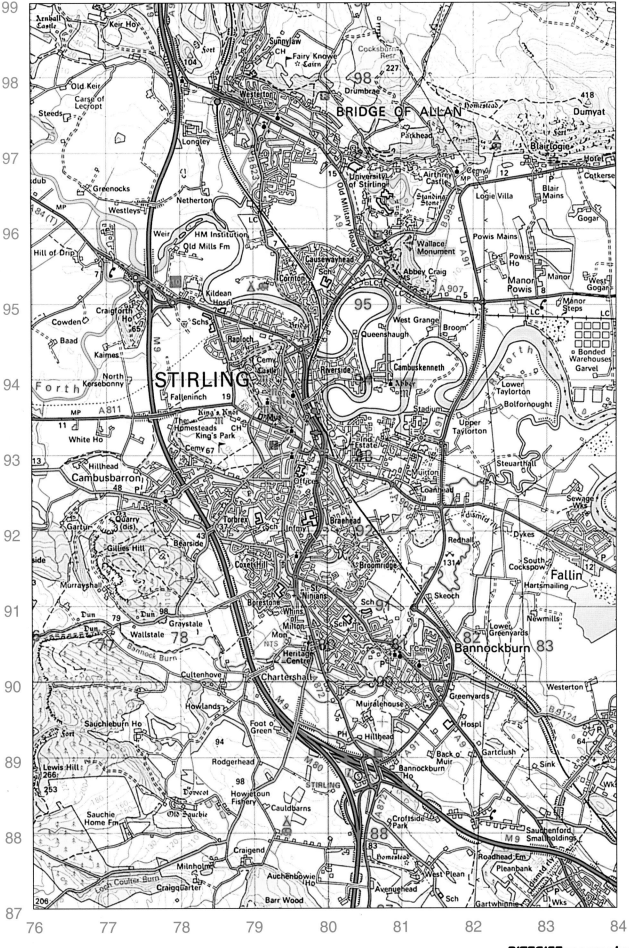

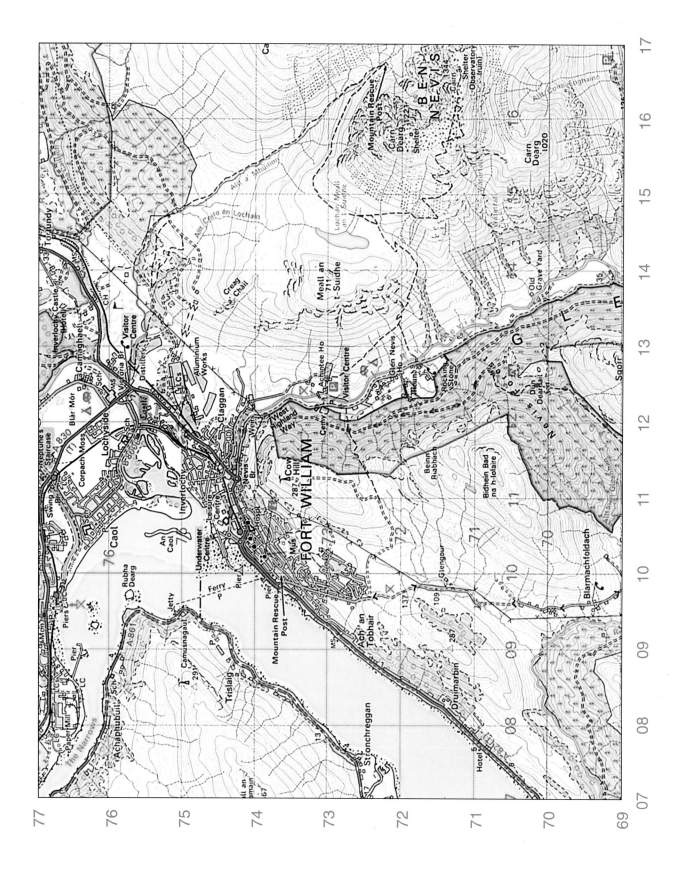

Key to Ordnance survey symbols

1:50 000

ROADS AND PATHS	VOIES DE COMMUNICATIONS
Not necessarily rights of way	VERKEHRSNETZ

Service area M 9   **Elevated**
(S)   **En Viaduc**
Junction number 10   **überhöht**

Motorway (dual carriageway)
Autoroute (chaussées separées) avec aire de service
et échangeur avec numero de l'échangeur
Autobahn (zweibahnig) mit Versorgungs - und
Anschlussstelle sowie Nummer der Anschlussstelle

Motorway under construction
Autoroute en construction
Autobahn im Bau

Unfenced   **Footbridge**
A 9 (T)   **Passerelle**
Fussgängerbrücke
Sans clôture   **Dual carriageway**
A 81   **Chaussées separées**
Zweibahnig

Trunk road
Route de grande circulation
Fernverkehrsstrasse

Main road
Route principale
Hauptstrasse

Main road under construction
Route principale en construction
Hauptstrasse im Bau

Uneingehegt
B 822

Secondary road
Route secondaire
Nebenstrasse

A 855   B 885

Narrow road with passing places
Route étroite avec voies de dépassement
Enge Strasse mit Ausweich-Überholstellen

Bridge
Pont
Brücke

Road generally more than 4 m wide
Route généralement de plus de 4 m de largeur
Strasse, Minimalbreite im allg. 4 m

Road generally less than 4 m wide
Route généralement de moins de 4 m de largeur
Strasse, Maximalbreite im allg. 4 m

Other road, drive or track
Autre route, allée ou sentier
Sonstige Strasse, Zufahrt oder Feldweg

Path   Sentier ·   Fussweg

Gradient : 1 in 5 and steeper   1 in 7 to 1 in 5
Pente : 20% et plus   de 14% à 20%
Steigungen : 20% und mehr   14% bis 20%

Gates   Road tunnel
Barrières   Tunnel routier
Schranken   Strassentunnel

Ferry P   **Ferry V**

Ferry (passenger)   Ferry (vehicle)
Bac pour piétons   Bac pour véhicules
Personenfähre   Autofähre

PUBLIC RIGHTS OF WAY
(Not applicable to Scotland)

DROIT DE PASSAGE PUBLIC
ÖFFENTLICHE WEGE

.... Footpath

---------- Bridleway

-·---·---·---·- Road used as a public path

-·+·+·+·+·+·+·- Byway open to all traffic

Public rights of way indicated by these symbols have been
derived from Definitive Maps as amended by later enactments
or instruments held by Ordnance Survey

RAILWAYS

▬▬▬	Track multiple or single	┼┼┼┼	Freight line, siding or tramway
┼┼┼┼	Track narrow gauge	○▭	Station (a) principal (b) closed to passengers
⫽⫽	Bridges, Footbridge	‖ LC	Level crossing
▨:::::▨	Tunnel	▒▒▒▒	Embankment
◠◡	Viaduct	▨▨▨▨	Cutting

General Information

LAND FEATURES

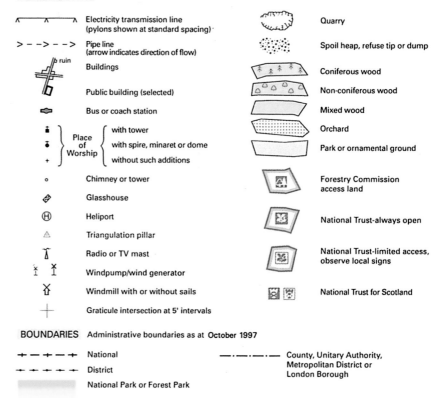

Electricity transmission line (pylons shown at standard spacing)	
Pipe line (arrow indicates direction of flow)	
Buildings	
Public building (selected)	
Bus or coach station	
Place of Worship — with tower	
Place of Worship — with spire, minaret or dome	
Place of Worship — without such additions	
Chimney or tower	
Glasshouse	
Heliport	
Triangulation pillar	
Radio or TV mast	
Windpump/wind generator	
Windmill with or without sails	
Graticule intersection at 5' intervals	

Quarry

Spoil heap, refuse tip or dump

Coniferous wood

Non-coniferous wood

Mixed wood

Orchard

Park or ornamental ground

Forestry Commission access land

National Trust-always open

National Trust-limited access, observe local signs

National Trust for Scotland

BOUNDARIES   Administrative boundaries as at October 1997

+ — + — +   National

+ — + — +   District

National Park or Forest Park

—·—·—   County, Unitary Authority, Metropolitan District or London Borough

TOURIST INFORMATION

RENSEIGNEMENTS TOURISTIQUES DIVERS
ALLGEMEINE TOURISTENANGABEN

ℹ ℹ Information centre, all year / seasonal
Bureau de renseignements, ouvert toute l'année / en saison
Informationsbüro, ganzjährlich / saisonal

Viewpoint
Point de vue
Aussichtspunkt

P Parking
Parking
Parkplatz

✕ Picnic site
Emplacement de pique-nique
Picknickplatz

⚑ Camp site
Terrain de camping
Campingplatz

Caravan site
Terrain pour caravanes
Wohnwagenplatz

▲ Youth hostel
Auberge de jeunesse
Jugendherberge

Selected places of tourist interest
Endroits d'un intérêt touristique particulier
Ausgesuchte Orte, von Interesse für Touristen

Telephone, public/motoring organisation
Téléphone, publique/associations automobiles
Telefon, öffentliches/Automobilklub

Golf course or links
Terrain de golf
Golfplatz

PC Public convenience (in rural areas)
WC (à la campagne)
Toiletten in ländlichen Gebieten

ROUTE OF WEST HIGHLAND WAY

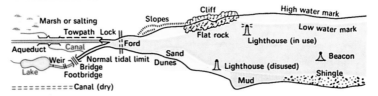

Drymen
Killearn

West Highland Way

Long Distance Route (LDR)
Itinéraire à Longue Distance
Fernverkehrsstrasse

WATER FEATURES

Marsh or salting
Towpath   Lock
Aqueduct   Canal   Ford
Weir   Normal tidal limit
Bridge
Lake   Footbridge
= = = = = = = = Canal (dry)

Slopes   Cliff   High water mark
Flat rock   Low water mark
Lighthouse (in use)
Sand   Dunes
Lighthouse (disused)   Beacon
Mud   Shingle